EVERYDAY GENIUS

FOCUSING ON
YOUR EMOTIONAL INTELLIGENCE

KEVIN FLANAGAN

First published in 1998 by
Marino Books
16 Hume Street Dublin 2
Tel: (01) 661 5299; Fax: (01) 661 8583;
e.mail: books@marino.ie

Trade enquiries to CMD Distribution
55A Spruce Avenue
Stillorgan Industrial Park Blackrock
County Dublin
Tel: (01) 294 2556; Fax: (01) 294 2564

© Kevin Flanagan 1998

ISBN 1 85635 063 6

10 9 8 7 6 5 4 3 2 1

A CIP record for this title is available
from the British Library

Cover design by
Penhouse Design Group
Printed in Ireland by ColourBooks
Baldoyle Industrial Estate, Dublin 13

ABOUT THE AUTHOR

Kevin Flanagan trained with Professor Eugene Gendlin at the Focusing Institute in Chicago. He is a registered Focusing Trainer and in 1997 was invited by Professor Gendlin to become a coordinator of the Focusing Institute in New York. Kevin now teaches the two-year professional training programme leading to certification with the Focusing Institute. He also trains groups in the Focusing method. He is Director of the Stress Clinic and author of the number one bestseller *Maximum Points – Minimum Panic.*

DEDICATION

I would like to dedicate this book to Professor Eugene
Gendlin and to Phil Kelly and Kathleen Kavanagh for
helping me discover Focusing and making possible an
extraordinary journey

ACKNOWLEDGEMENTS

I would like to thank Peter Campbell, Ed McMahon and
all I have met on my Focusing journey around the world,
including Brigitte. Plus a special word for Ciarán and
Mairéad, Anne and Eileen, Paul and Emma, Spencer and
of course Alan and the Marines (many of whom are now
sadly missing in action!). They all make my life rich and
full of fun.

Also Anne and Jo at Marino, Iris and Donncha at
Trinity College, Dublin. All at Blazing Salads. Emma and
the staff at the Shelbourne Hotel, Duly at Friarsland and
Martin Kane. Finally, a special word of thanks to Lourda.

Contents

FOREWORD

I welcome Kevin Flanagan's new book. It includes one of
the best personal descriptions of the Focusing process
that I have ever read. It makes clear how to get beyond
the first level of feelings that most people know, and
beyond the murky zone beneath those. He shows how
different it is to attend to what comes in the centre of
the body. The book will help many people to discover
Focusing and to improve many other activities by doing
them – to use the author's own words – with 'the sense
of being talked to by something down there that is not
infected by our own fears and conditioning'.

Professor Eugene Gendlin PhD

PROLOGUE: WHAT IS GENIUS?

Genius Pl. genii [a. L. genius, to beget, Gr. to be born]

a) In classical pagan belief: The god or attending spirit allotted to every person at birth, who governs their fortunes, moulds their character and finally leads them out of this world and into the next.

b) One who is possessed of a particular kind of creative power which appears to proceed from supernatural inspiration and which produces miraculous results.

c) One who is touched by God.

From time immemorial, certain individuals have been able to create great works of art – a classical Greek temple, a Roman aqueduct, an illuminated medieval manuscript, a soaring Gothic cathedral, a piece of Renaissance sculpture or a painting like the *Mona Lisa*. Nowadays this talent might be found just as well in the design of a spacecraft or a microchip. The individuals who create great art and ideas are called geniuses and it seems that all are touched in a special way; some believe they are touched directly by the divine.

The Romans believed that genius was a spirit given to the individual soul at birth. Its job was to guide them successfully through life and to show them their 'divinely appointed path'. But the Romans believed that everyone was blessed with this guiding spirit, not just rare individuals. Everyone was touched by genius.

In this century behavioural science (the serious study of human behaviour and what makes people act in the way they do) has started to uncover evidence of this 'guiding spirit within'. Psychologists like C. J. Jung, Carl Rogers and Eugene Gendlin have discovered ways in which the human psyche operates and have identified an 'inner form of guidance'.

It may well be that they are uncovering for us the lost voice of our individual genius and giving us the opportunity to experience once again this inner guiding spirit – a spirit we all possess, but that has been forgotten. This book is designed to outline their discoveries and to help you discover your own unique guiding spirit – your own genius.

INTRODUCTION

Let us first look at some of the definitions and objectives of this book, starting with the title *Everyday Genius*. This finds its definition in the Roman idea that at birth we are each given a guiding spirit that helps us through life, moulding our character and enlightening our understanding. This spirit stays with us till our death, when it guides us into the next world. The idea of a guiding spirit recurs in Christianity with the concept of the guardian angel, in this case the bearer of a message of guidance. The word 'angel' is derived from the Greek word for messenger.

Then there is the phrase 'emotional intelligence': 'emotional' referring to 'feeling' and 'intelligence' to the 'facility of understanding'. Emotional intelligence means understanding feeling.

It seems to me that modern behavioural science is beginning to show us just how 'genius' works and how this 'guiding spirit' may be understood to talk to human beings. The work of Professor Eugene Gendlin in particular is starting to show us just how inspiration and the internal problem-solving mechanism works. Gendlin has already identified a particular internal process that takes place when humans successfully solve their own emotional problems. He calls it *Focusing*. What's more, Gendlin has discovered that this process can be taught. It is now possible to click into the problem-solving mechanism and start this internal process of emotional resolution at will.

Research shows that Focusing solves not only our emotional dilemmas but our creative ones, be they in work or in relationships. Focusing, as Gendlin defines it, *works*. And it will add enormously to your life. The fact that it may also connect you to the transcendent is a bonus.

THINKING VERSUS FEELING
THE FUNDAMENTAL FACTS

When making important decisions in life we do so on the basis of our emotions and *not* intellectually or rationally as was previously supposed. Research shows that when we are confronted with an important decision, say leaving a love partner, we will first consult how we *feel* about that person and then make up our minds based on that feeling. It will be a complex, holistic and emotional decision based on a gut feeling that will determine our course of action.

Immediately the decision is made – say to leave the partner – we will *rationalise* it and come up with all the intellectual and cognitive reasons why we should leave our partner. We will then use them when we are talking to him or her.

That is why it is impossible for departing lovers ever to explain adequately to their 'ex' the reasons why they are leaving. It is probable that they do not fully understand them themselves. What's more, they will never really be able to sum up the deep-seated emotional feeling that has led to the decision, which is by its very nature non-verbal. The fact is that *reason* will have had little to do with their coming to that decision; emotion and gut feeling were what mattered.

THE SOUL OF MODERN MAN AND THE NEW PHYSICS

Until quite recently it was not possible for science to talk about such things as a man's soul – that was left to religion. But this was not always the case: the great divide began during the Age of Reason, when the dominance of religion was questioned and the empirical scientific approach gradually took over as a way of proving how things worked. Previous to that, all creation was explained by divine revelation. It was in the Age of Reason that the divide between mind and spirit and body and soul had its origins. There was a tacit agreement between science and religion that the Church would look after men's souls while science would look after their minds and their material needs.

One of the first and most notable victims of this schism was medicine, which began to become purely mechanistic in its approach to disease, whereas previously it had taken into account the emotional and spiritual state of the person. Medical opinion today tends to view illness exclusively in mechanical or genetic terms. Until recently, emotional issues were not acknowledged as having any serious bearing on disease. (One of the reasons for this was that emotional states were considered impossible to measure until the development of behavioural science.) It is only in the last few years that the emotional element of sickness has been acknowledged. Being emotionally well (which comes also from being emotionally intelligent and aware) is a fundamental requirement for good health and one that we will be examining in this book. Research shows that acquiring skills such as Focusing and empathetic listening dramatically improves your emotional well-being and physical health!

In this book you will learn:

- how to focus
- how to listen empathetically

Extensive research has shown that these skills will:

- improve your emotional intelligence
- maintain and improve your physical health

PART 1

THE DISCOVERY OF FOCUSING AND LISTENING

1

LISTENING TO THE VOICE OF YOUR GENIUS

One of the discoveries of behavioural science is the inner voice, the voice of knowing, that tells us exactly what we should do. It is a quiet, gentle voice that suggests a course of action that is remarkable for its appropriateness. This voice counsels us to take steps that promote resolution and development in life.

The voice seems to come from a separate entity. It is not so much 'me' (the person who is currently overwhelmed by life's problems) but another who speaks to me, the 'ever watchful witness' who is heard in the space between my thoughts or in the moments of quiet reflection when I sit in silence with myself. Then I sense it, behind all the chatter, a presence that seems always to have been there.

HOW TO LISTEN TO THIS INNER VOICE

'Focusing' was first defined by Professor Eugene Gendlin, who has spent a lifetime studying people's inner processes. It means taking complex and unclear emotional feelings and giving them a special sort of attention until they become clear to us. Gendlin developed the concept of Focusing as a result of over thirty years' research into therapy in general and psychotherapy in particular. The aim of his research was to show exactly how 'successful' therapy worked.

His was an extraordinary discovery, because up until then therapy had had an alarming failure rate. Far more people failed in therapy than succeeded. It seemed that very few people were able to listen to their inner guiding voice. In the end Gendlin was able to identify what successful people actually did in therapy and he called this process 'Focusing'.

So what is Focusing?

On one level Focusing is a *bodily felt* way of knowing and assessing a situation or a problem, one that is ruled not by the intellect or reason but by intuition or gut feeling. This visceral (gut) feeling is almost unconscious; it knows something, but that something may be unclear to the conscious mind, like a vague or uneasy feeling in the body. That is until you focus on it. Then everything starts to become clear.

Here is an example of the most basic form of Focusing.

SOMETHING'S WRONG BUT I DON'T KNOW WHAT

Imagine you leave the house in the morning and are in the car going to work. You are ten minutes into your journey and well into the morning traffic. Suddenly you get an uncomfortable feeling that you have forgotten to do something important in the house but you cannot remember what it is. As you wait at the traffic lights your whole body fills with tension. You feel butterflies in your tummy and a tightness in your chest as you rack your mind in search of the missing item.

'What was it?' you say to yourself, as you go over a list in your mind. 'Did I switch off the gas? Yes. Lock the door? Yes. Turn off the immersion heater? Yes.'

You cannot recall what it is and think about turning back but you're stuck in traffic and it means you will be late for work so you try to dismiss the nagging worry from your mind. 'I'm probably only imagining it!' you say, and continue to drive on, hoping the nagging feeling will go away.

But the feeling that something important has been left undone continues to trouble you. You try to be positive and whistle a tune but it does not go away. You turn on the radio and try to listen to the morning show but it does not go away. You reach over and light a cigarette and for a few minutes feel good as the nicotine produces a temporary flood of relief, but after five minutes this too wears off and the tense feeling starts to creep back into your stomach again, putting you on edge. If anything the feeling is worse than before.

Eventually you begin pleading with the queasy feeling that is gnawing at your insides. 'Look!' you say to it. 'I'm almost at work now. If I turn back I'm going to be hours late and get into trouble with the boss. Surely it can wait!' But the feeling does not go away; it is growing stronger the further away from home you get.

Finally you can stand it no more and you pull in, stop the car and begin to attend seriously to the tense feeling inside. Unbeknown to yourself, you have begun to perform a type of Focusing – focusing on the uneasy feeling inside.

You take a deep breath and bring your attention to the tension churning in your stomach. 'Now what is it?' you ask as you close your eyes and begin to focus on the queasy feeling, going over all the possible items that you could have left undone.

Was it the back door? Did I lock it? You check this possibility against the churning feeling in your stomach. It's still churning so it can't have been that.

Was it the bedroom window? You have left that open before. No, the feeling is still there, making you anxious and on edge.

Your mind goes on and on, deeper and deeper, till suddenly it makes contact with the unconscious knowing that something is wrong. And then you strike gold! You can now *see* what your body *knew* all along but somehow could not quite tell you. It is the family cat that you forgot to put out. Your partner usually feeds it and puts it out but this morning she got up and left early, shouting up to you as you were still half-asleep not to forget to put the cat out. (Last time it was locked in it ruined an expensive rug and wrecked the front room trying to get out.)

Great physical relief accompanies this discovery. Suddenly the terrible tension in your body melts away. The sick feeling in your gut disappears, as does the tightness in your throat. You smile and begin to laugh with relief, banging the steering wheel with your hand at your stupidity but happy that you have finally tracked the missing item down.

The warning feelings would not give up. The unconscious bodily feeling knew you had to do something and it would not give up until you had recognised it, however hard you tried to dismiss it. Its main means of achieving this was to subject your body to almost unbearable tension until you stopped and took the time to track down the issue – until your mind discovered what your body already knew.

Now that your body has alerted you to the danger of the cat, you are in a position to do something to remedy the problem. You can take action – phone a neighbour or return to the house yourself. You can even decide to take no action and live with the consequences – but that's all right. The body has done what it had to do and warned you. It can rest now – and it does.

DISTRUST OF THE BODY

On this occasion, the way you got to hear this unconscious message was by focusing on strong bodily feelings. Unfortunately, because our education system does not honour (or even acknowledge) this form of bodily intelligence, we do not get the opportunity to use it. Developments such as Focusing, which enhance our emotional or intuitive intelligence, are not as widely known or used as they should be, because our conditioned reflex is to rely on our intellect.

The reason for this is complex and has deep roots in history. It is partly due to the early Fathers of the Church and their suspicion of the human body. Philosophers like St Augustine taught that the human body was essentially 'sinful' and not to be trusted. Some of the early church-men believed that the human body – far from being a miracle of creation – was the home of the devil!

As a result of this attitude, a pathological distrust of the human body, sometimes bordering on hatred, developed. We see this harsh attitude exemplified in the brutal practices of mortifying the flesh, which included flagellation, starving the body of foods and liquids and exposing it to extremes of heat or cold or to long periods without sleep. All this despite the fact that the body is said to be 'the temple of the Holy Spirit' and made 'in the image of God'!

The effect of this attitude to the body has been to make people distrust the very home in which they live their earthly life. It is an extraordinary attitude given what we now know about the miracle of the human body. It has led also to an almost pathological attitude towards sexuality and a denial of our deepest evolutionary sexual instincts – instincts that were given specifically to ensure the survival of the human race.

The legacy of this hatred of the body remains with us today and is seen in our distrust of our bodily intelligence – the body's ability to know things – and our over-reliance on reason and the cognitive functions of the brain to solve our problems.

Now behavioural science is unlocking the amazing secrets of the body and showing us exactly how intricate and sophisticated it is.

2

BODILY SENSED INTELLIGENCE

The discoveries of behavioural science show that the human body is more sophisticated than we have ever imagined. Furthermore, it is becoming increasingly clear that the body houses many different forms of intelligence or ways of knowing. And this whole body cognition or way of knowing can be very powerful and useful.

Already scientists have found neuropeptides in the stomach lining similar to those found in the brain, giving a possible explanation as to why we experience so many strong emotions as gut feelings and not thoughts in the head. It seems as if the centre of the body acts almost like a second brain, providing the human organism with a whole additional range of information.

Take a moment to notice and list all the different ways in which you receive, sense or feel information – especially emotional information. Do these experiences come to you as thoughts in your head or feelings in your body? Check your own experience of where you feel the following emotions in your body:

- love
- hatred
- a feeling that something is going to happen
- a sudden dread or fear that all is not well
- an uplifting feeling that all will be well despite the evidence of your reason
- a deep conviction that you should take particular steps or actions
- a sense that you are fulfilling your destiny
- a deep sense that you have met a person who is going to play an important role in your life

INTUITIVE INTELLIGENCE

What characterises all the above forms of intelligence or knowing is:

- how they are physically felt in the body (and not just thought of as ideas in the head)
- how they largely bypass reason and go straight to the core of a person's knowing, where they are apprehended directly

The word for this form of intelligence is *intuitive*.

Take a moment to list your experience of your own intuitive intelligence: occasions when you receive and act on information without having to resort to analysis, cognition, logical appraisal or intellectual reasoning.

For example, you might say that you rely largely on your intuitive intelligence when you decide to embark on a relationship with someone, change jobs or even move house. Creative acts like writing, sculpting, painting, acting and playing music could not be successful without the use of intuitive intelligence. When we really examine our lives we find that most of our major decisions are taken on the basis of a gut feeling.

Jot down how you came to make your own decisions on the following things. Which did you rely on most – pure reason or intuitive insight?

- marrying or setting up with my life partner
- choosing my current career
- starting a major relationship
- ending a major relationship
- leaving one job for another
- starting or ending a friendship
- deciding to emigrate
- buying my house

Many will answer that intuitive and gut feelings played a large part in their decision-making process. But what exactly is this intuitive intelligence and how can we readily find it?

THE HEAD DOES NOT KNOW EVERYTHING

First let us examine the example given in the previous chapter, of having forgotten to put out the cat; for, simple as it may seem, it shows us many aspects of this newly researched bodily sensed intelligence.

The person intuitively knew that he had somehow forgotten to do something. But while his body knew this and kept issuing warning distress signals, his mind did not readily accept them.

The example shows how we automatically turn to our head to solve our problems, even when it was our bodily felt intuitive intelligence that alerted us to the problem in the first place! We rely first and foremost on our intellect to figure out what is bothering our body, and not on the body itself. We do this as a reflex action because we have been programmed to solve most of our problems with our left-brained, cognitive and rational thinking processes. We have been educated to put this form of thinking above all others, at the expense of focused intelligence, which is based on intuitive and bodily felt knowing.

But the head does not know everything. Often the body knows things more clearly and more accurately. In the example it took a long time for the person to get in contact with his bodily felt knowing. This is typical behaviour for almost all of us. First we use our head to attempt to figure out what is wrong. It tries but fails, for it is really much better at performing sequential, rational and cognitive tasks. Because we have not been educated to know about focused bodily felt intelligence, however, we have to continue to use our intellectual facilities to decipher a physical signal that something is wrong. As the mind cannot come up with an answer it naturally tries another tack.

First it tries to dismiss the body: 'You're wrong!' it tells it. 'You're only imagining it.' But the intuitive bodily knowing won't go away and keeps on sending out the distress signal.

Secondly, the mind tries to distract the person, in this case prompting him to turn on the car radio. But this does not work either; the intuitive bodily knowing that something is wrong will not be distracted!

Next, the mind tries numbing the body with chemicals, in this case nicotine. This is a highly effective solution in the short term as it chemically removes the stress feeling, flooding the brain with 'happiness hormones' while the needs of the addiction are temporarily met. But the effects of the cigarette last no more than a few minutes and soon the stress chemicals come flooding back, warning the body that something is amiss. It will not give up. Intuitive knowing produces an actual chemical response that is physically felt in the body.

The reasoning capacities of the left brain admit partial defeat and it begins to bargain with the bodily felt intuitive feelings. 'OK!' it says. 'We know something's up, but we can't do anything about it right now. Look, we'll be late and get into terrible trouble if we turn around and go home now. Please forget about it just this time!'

But the body will not let go until the problem is solved. The mind has to deal with it directly, engaging it in the process of Focusing. Then together, like deep sea divers, the body and the head delve the depths of the bodily felt knowing until the mind discovers what it has been looking for (and what the body, through its intuitive intelligence, has known all along).

3

THE MISSING LINK

Eugene Gendlin seems to have discovered the mechanism that decodes intuitive bodily felt intelligence. Focusing is the missing link between our reason and our unconscious.

It is Focusing that allows our minds to see what our body already knows.

As such it is a phenomenally useful process. The fact that it can be learnt makes it even more exciting. Learning Focusing is almost like getting the use of another form of intelligence, having the use of a second brain.

In Gendlin's research on those who had a successful outcome from therapy, he discovered that these people processed their problems in a very particular way, characterised by:

1 first recognising that the problem actually exists
2 then getting a physically felt sense of the problem, how the body actually carries the burden of the problem, like a 'knot in the tummy' or 'weight on the shoulders'
3 then allowing this bodily felt sense to symbolise itself and spontaneously produce an image of itself, for

example, 'I now see the feeling inside as a black cloud overhead blotting out the light'

4 now conversing with the feeling symbolised by the 'black cloud overhead blotting out the light' and asking it questions

The first question concerns the past history of the problem and how it has concretely affected the client's life. The second question concerns the future, and what needs to happen for the problem to be solved.

While Focusing on the problem in this specific way and asking these particular questions of the problem (as it is felt in the body and not thought of in the brain), the client awaits the answers.

Finally comes the Focusing insight. From somewhere deep inside the body, from the actual place where the pain of the problem is felt, comes the answer. It is felt not as an idea that has come as the result of logical calculation but as a sudden insight, a flash of inspiration that illuminates the confusion inside in such a way that the road ahead is suddenly clear. For this lightning flash of insight has also illuminated the obstacles that stand in the way of progress, so that the client can see the way ahead and choose action steps that will take him to the solution.

This is the miracle that is at the core of Focusing: an answer to the problem materialises spontaneously into consciousness. And the answer comes primarily not from rational analysis but from intuitive insight. One has an answer where before there was confusion and that answer is:

- fresh
- surprising
- uniquely appropriate
- helpful
- complete with an action step

WHAT HAPPENS INSIDE THE HUMAN BODY WHEN A FOCUSING INSIGHT OCCURS

Current research shows that several physiological events take place inside the body and brain of the person who is experiencing a Focusing insight. The left and right hemispheres of the brain produce unique and congruent brainwave patterns as the resolution arises. There is a shift in several physiological indicators including:

- heartbeat
- blood pressure
- immune system response
- muscular tension

This is followed by a flood of physically felt relief that is chemically transmitted, and a sense of profound well-being permeates the body.

It seems that Focusing opens up the physiological and psychological problem-solving mechanism inherent in the human body. And whether the problem is physical or emotional, it seems that Focusing is the process that helps provide the answer. It is the core of the body's problem-solving mechanism.

Some would maintain that Focusing is the inherent

'problem-solving process' – the process that decodes the intuitive, bodily felt feelings in the human body and makes them accessible to the human mind.

THE FOCUSING INSIGHT
NATURE'S ANSWER TO MANKIND'S PROBLEMS

But why should there be an internal mechanism that helps solve the complex problems of mankind? The answer to this is that nature designed it that way. It does not want any organism to get stuck in the mud – this does not serve evolution, which is always striving to help every organism reach its full potential.

One can see this helpful mechanism at work on many levels – from nature working to help simple one-cell organisms evolve, to a way of knowing, like Focusing, that helps highly complex human beings overcome their problems.

Many commentators believe that Focusing and other tools for inner exploring – like 'client centred' work and Gestalt – are actually spiritual pathways to understanding the divine elements within us. Many 'enlightened' religious people are now studying such disciplines and using them to find their own way to the source of their being.

Even Carl Rogers, who spent his whole life keeping the word 'God' out of his research and teaching, was forced to admit at the end of his life that the process of inner healing seemed to involve something profoundly spiritual and transcendent.

SCIENCE AND THE 'GOD' WORD

In our efforts to be scientific we sometimes react violently against the old belief systems and consequently throw the baby out with the bathwater.

Perhaps the reason many people find Focusing so spiritual is the fact that it echoes the ancient ideas of a personal genius or an inner guiding spirit. It also echoes the Christian idea of a guardian angel or messenger, otherwise known as *conscience*.

Is it possible to suppose that Focusing is part of the process by which our guiding spirit talks to us? The parallels between the intuitive Focusing voice and the traditional and spiritual voice of our conscience are remarkable. In both cases a quiet inner voice whispers solutions to us directly, bypassing reason. Both seem to be separate from our ego, to stand outside desires and emotions and observe our actions dispassionately. And most importantly, both seem to offer solutions not from the head, with its old and often outworn ideas, but from somewhere much freer. Somewhere that is not pre-occupied with self-aggrandisement or score settling. Somewhere where wisdom and sanity reign.

It may well be that Gendlin has helped identify the inner voice of conscience as it resides in the human psyche. We can certainly conclude that he has discovered a tool that helps us profoundly in dealing with emotional and creative problems of every sort. There is little doubt that learning Focusing (and its sister, empathetic listening) will add greatly to your life.

4
—

USING THE BODY'S SECOND BRAIN

Extensive research shows that Focusing is like plugging into a second brain – the body's brain. This helps you to:

- find intuitive answers to your emotional problems directly and efficiently, revealing why you are often stuck for years with the same old gripes and weaknesses
- listen effectively to the stressful feelings that so often assail our bodies, leaving them prone to every kind of stress-related illness, from heart disease to cancer
- solve creative problems, from writing business reports to penning novels
- understand why we suffer from certain emotional problems, such as low self-esteem, anxiety attacks and anger outbursts

FOCUSING – RESEARCHED AND CLINICALLY PROVEN

As Focusing came out of the scientific study of therapy, it is uniquely well placed to solve our personal problems. Professor Gendlin was keen from the outset to see if it could be taught to ordinary people who did not have an understanding of the esoteric language of therapy. He found that Focusing could be taught and learnt by virtually anyone.

As a result, people now have a researched and clinically proven tool or process with which to tackle life's problems. Focusing has been the subject of thirty years of research and experimental work, both at the University of Chicago and at university behavioural science departments worldwide. Now Gendlin's Focusing work and research are used in therapy all over the world and their influence is increasing.

CURRENT FOCUSING RESEARCH

The research is growing apace and evolving into different areas, from successful clinical trials showing how Focusing ameliorates pain in chronic migraine sufferers, to dozens of studies showing how Focusing helps different forms of therapy work more effectively by allowing the client to feel the body's intelligence.

FOCUSING AS 'SELF-THERAPY'

In this respect Gendlin has made a profound contribution to the area of safe self-therapy. Therapy has always been kept in the hands of the 'Men in White' – the assorted collection of psychologists, psychiatrists, psychotherapists and doctors who have traditionally tended to the mentally and emotionally ill.

But there has always been a problem with this.

DISEMPOWERING

For one thing, this attitude is disempowering, presuming as it does that an expert is able to solve our problems when we cannot. As both Jung and Rogers pointed out, it is well-nigh impossible for one human being fully to understand the predicament of another, let alone prescribe specific behavioural help. Often the very sickness itself is found in our willingness to hand over our personal responsibility to others, be they therapists or counsellors, just as smokers hand over responsibility for their health to doctors, hoping they will remedy an illness that is one hundred per cent avoidable.

WHAT HAPPENS IN THERAPY

Research at the University of Chicago shows that a lot of therapy simply does not work. In fact it was the poor performance of therapy that prompted Gendlin to initiate his research in the first place.

A key reason for therapy going wrong was that clients stayed in their heads and tried to solve their problems cognitively and rationally rather than referring to the way in which their bodies held the problems.

Gendlin's research also showed what went right in the therapeutic process. What characterised successful clients was their ability to address problems in their bodies and allow the visceral feeling of the problems to open up and offer solutions.

Why Focusing Works

It seems that feeling the problem as it is held in the body allows a solution to arise spontaneously from the unconscious. This solution works far better than any worked out in the head or prescribed by a so-called 'expert'.

Some people who know Focusing believe it is the process by which we communicate with the divine, now analysed by behavioural science for the first time. While I was studying Focusing with Professor Gendlin in Chicago, I had the opportunity to ask him about this particular point and I found his response illuminating. He felt it did not matter what words you used to describe things – the truth was that the Focusing process *worked*. Many replicated studies have shown over the years that Focusing is not a New Age fad or the next Californian psychobabble fashion – it is science. I would invite you to read the research that has been done on Focusing, starting with Professor Gendlin's own impressive work and his book *Focusing*.

But perhaps the most important thing about Focusing is that it is your own unique process by which you get to the bottom of your own truth. You do not need a guru or a leader, just someone who knows the process and can explain it to you – as in this book. Then you can take the Focusing process away and start to work with it yourself, sharing it with a loved one or friend.

You will be getting valuable insights *from yourself – to yourself.*

Now we can go on and begin to learn more about this inner process that Carl Rogers called 'an invaluable tool'.

5

CARL ROGERS AND EMPATHETIC LISTENING

Traditionally we have accessed the guiding awareness within by consulting special members of the tribe or community who are held to be in touch with this spirit. Originally it was the shaman or priest; now it is more likely to be the psychotherapist, psychiatrist, counsellor or healer.

We also use prayer and dreams to elicit this guidance when we are faced with a major problem or dilemma in life. Then we have direct experience of the guiding spirit, in such forms as conscience, intuition and inspiration (which means 'breathing in the spirit').

BEHAVIOURAL SCIENCE
THE PATH TO SPIRITUAL ENLIGHTENMENT

Today in many ways behavioural science is doing the job that religion and philosophy once did. It is actually studying 'what makes people tick' and examining that profoundly mysterious place – the seat of the emotions or the soul.

Carl Jung was one of the first philosopher-psychologists to pursue this path openly. He was quite clear that modern man was lost and desperately looking for his soul. Jung believed that until he found it, mankind was in grave danger of self-annihilation.

Carl Rogers and Eugene Gendlin came from a different culture and indeed a different era, even though their lifetimes overlapped with Jung's. Jung spoke in the traditional, richly cultural voice of Europe, while Rogers and Gendlin spoke through the newer, fresher voice of America. Essentially, though, they were all seeking to understand what made man tick and why he behaved in the way he did. In the end, Rogers and Gendlin built on the foundations laid by Jung as they got closer to uncovering the truth.

LISTENING FOR THE ANSWER WITHIN

Carl Rogers is one of the great unsung heroes of the twentieth century. I say 'unsung', because he is still largely unknown to the general population, even though he changed the way therapy is conducted. Anyone who undergoes therapy nowadays, of whatever kind, will be reaping some of the benefits of Rogers's work.

Rogers was one of the first people to bring proper research procedures to the realm of human behaviour. He was one of the first 'modern' behavioural scientists, and he strove all his life to justify his work by exposing it to the rigours of scientific analysis (though nowadays there are those who would question the validity of some of his scientific methods).

WHAT CARL ROGERS DISCOVERED

Carl Rogers discovered that if you allowed a human being to be truly heard, without judging him or weighing him down with advice, he would begin to discover the cause of his problem – and the solution – for *himself!*

It may not sound so now, but in the 1950s, when Rogers was making these discoveries, this opinion was considered revolutionary. Before Rogers, therapy consisted largely of analysis and prescriptive advice. Patients were analysed by doctors or psychiatrists and told (a) what was wrong with them, and (b) what they should do. It was assumed that only an 'expert' knew the answer, and in many cases drugs, in the form of pills, were considered the remedy.

Rogers turned all that on its head. He maintained that all human beings knew the solutions to their own unique problems. He also maintained that the very idea of an 'expert' in a white coat, telling people what to do, was misguided and disempowering in itself. He believed that only the clients themselves could know the full extent of their problem, because only they had experienced all the pain and the damage it had caused.

He had an optimistic view of human nature, believing that man was intrinsically able to find the answers to his own problems. It only required that the therapist listen to the client with total empathy, putting aside any personal judgement or advice, for the client to come slowly to his own resolution of the problem.

But this approach got Rogers into trouble with all sorts of people, from Fundamental Christians and the established churches to other therapeutic schools – all of whom viewed human nature differently, believing man to be flawed and weak and in need of firm guidance and strict, even totalitarian, control.

'EMPATHETIC LISTENING' – THE KEY TO SUCCESSFUL THERAPY

Rogers's research showed that successful therapy came through empathetic listening. Empathetic listening is where you listen not only to the meaning of the words that a person is speaking, but also to how it must feel for the person to say those words. To listen empathetically is to get inside the skin of another human being.

To do this you must:

- put aside your own judgement of the person being heard and how he or she is coping with the situation
- put aside your own opinion as to what the person should do in the situation
- listen totally to what the person is saying
- repeat back the key things the person says, using his or her own words wherever possible

ADVICE IS NOT ALWAYS HELPFUL

In order for the therapeutic process to take place, Rogers discovered that it was vital that the therapist refrain from telling his client what he or she should do. This only disempowered the person even more, making him or her come to rely on the therapist for direction and perhaps reinforcing the cycle of dependent behaviour that had disabled the client in the first place.

When people were heard in this empathetic way, Rogers observed that several remarkable things started to happen. Clients could begin to get a clear picture of the true state they were in – the full extent of the mess! Previous to that it had been hidden behind a wall of effort, while they desperately tried to follow the advice of friends, family or therapists, often to such an extent that they lost sight of the true problem. It would be like trying to concentrate on doing an exam while all your friends, family and teachers were gathered around your desk shouting advice. You would not do a good paper!

But if you were left on your own, in total peace and quiet, and given time, then slowly you could begin to examine the problems in front of you and come up with your own analysis out of which solutions might arise.

EXPERIENCING LIFE FOR OURSELVES

I cannot live your life for you, neither can you live mine. But we are very quick to suggest to people how they should live their lives. Look at your own experience. Have you noticed how easy it is to sort out the problems of a friend or relative? 'You should tell the boss to get lost!' or 'If I were you I would get out of that relationship today!'

It is so easy to sit with friends and sort out all their problems for them; and then to sit in judgement when they do not follow your well-intentioned advice, and say, 'I told you so.'

But have you noticed that when you yourself get advice over a personal problem of your own and your friend tells you to leave your job/wife/boyfriend/son/work/old friend/grumpy relative ... it is suddenly not so easy to follow the advice and drop the relationship? Why is that?

EASY SOLUTIONS – DIFFICULT PROBLEMS

The reason is simple. It is easy to solve other people's problems because we only ever get the most superficial idea of what the problem is really like.

It may seem obvious that your best friend's wife is cruel and uncaring and that he should get out of the marriage, take the two kids with him and set up on his

43

own. But you have no real idea of all the complex, unconscious forces that are at work in the mind and soul of your friend; or what it is like to suffer his own particular 'lows' (low self-esteem, for example). Nor are you taking into account the nature of the complex and often contradictory state that many of us call 'love'.

You do not wake up in his bed and get into his clothes each morning and lead his life. Neither can you really know what is going on deep in his heart and in his emotions for the woman that he has shared his life with and who has given birth to his children.

You cannot know fully all that he is feeling for another very good reason – he himself may not know fully why he cannot leave this apparently abusive relationship!

'UNCONSCIOUS' FEELINGS

Most of our deep emotional character stays hidden in our unconscious – as does most of the childhood conditioning that formed us.

We remain a mystery even to ourselves, unless we are intra-personally intelligent (having the ability to understand our own emotions) or lucky enough to meet friends who will really listen to us empathetically. Or we might come across good psychotherapy or a self-awareness technique like Focusing.

So it is hardly surprising that 'advice' – however well-intentioned – does not usually help. And worse: bad things can come from it. Strongly worded advice may get in the way of people finally getting to the root of their own problems and finding their own solutions.

44

In the end Rogers discovered that only the individual human psyche is capable of understanding the full complexity of its own intricate problem. Only it is wise enough to come up with the solution. It can be helped, and empathetic listening seems to help greatly.

WHAT HAPPENS DURING EMPATHETIC LISTENING

Several things happen during empathetic listening. The person gets distance from the overwhelming problem. He or she starts off by being overwhelmed by the problem and may feel that there is no hope of a solution. This is very debilitating and potentially dangerous.

Think back to your own experience of being overwhelmed by a personal problem or feeling. Take a moment to remember exactly how it felt when you were overwhelmed by a sense of abandonment or hopelessness, when someone had died or left you. Take a few seconds to get a flavour of that feeling. You can jot down the key words that describe how you felt in the space below.

How I Felt when I Was Overwhelmed by Difficult Feelings

- ....
- ....
- ....
- ....

Did it feel like any of the following?

- I felt trapped like an animal.
- Everything looked black.
- Hope receded. There seemed no point in going on.
- It felt like it would never get better.

Being overwhelmed can cause people to give up. It can also lead to a feeling of extreme isolation, and in that isolation the feelings seem to get worse. From feeling a little sad, you become sadness itself. And just as you thought the whole world was happy when you were in love, so now it feels as if the whole world is sad and a terrible place to be in. But this is just where empathetic listening comes into its own and helps.

'IT' AND 'ME'
GETTING DISTANCE FROM THE PROBLEM

When you are listened to empathetically, you start to talk about the problem, referring to it as 'it'. For example, instead of feeling totally overwhelmed by grief, you say things like, 'It's like I'm locked in a dark room – I can see no way to get out of it. It's a terrible feeling! And I don't seem to be able to do anything about it.'

This is actually the beginning of something very beneficial, because by referring to the problem as 'it', you are already putting distance between yourself and the problem. It is out there and you are over here talking about it. You are no longer all of the problem, there is a part of you that can see 'it' and talk about 'it'.

All the research shows that getting distance from a previously overwhelming problem is a fundamental first step in finding a solution and getting well again. Empathetic listening scores very highly on this point. It allows people to explore their feelings from a safe distance. In this way they begin to form a picture in their minds of what the problem is. Repeating to them the things they have just said helps them get a picture of their true state, in the same way as looking in the mirror helps you see exactly how you look, so that you can adjust your tie or hair.

THE IMPORTANCE OF 'MIRRORING'

If you were going on an important date or to a crucial meeting, would you rely totally on what a friend said about your appearance or would you want to check for yourself in the mirror? It is the same with reflective empathetic listening (when you say back to the person what they have just said). This form of listening creates a mirror in which the person can see their exact feelings and the emotional clothes they are wearing. On hearing it repeated, they are able to see their own emotional landscape just as it is – and not as someone else sees it.

Just check your own experience. It does not matter if a dozen friends say, 'You look great!' if you do not feel it yourself. Only you know what feels right on you, just as only you know what feels right inside.

SEEING YOUR REALITY IN THE MIRROR

All the research shows that confronting reality is the first step – the primary foundation for permanent and effective healing. (Reality is all important. When you know the stairs at home are rotten and about to fall down you can do something about it. Pretending they are safe will not make walking up them any less dangerous!)

Empathetic listening helps people discover the reality of how they are feeling. Once they have done that they can begin the exploration which will lead to action steps and resolution.

BEING OVERWHELMED BY THE PROBLEM

TALKING IT THROUGH LETS YOU SEE YOURSELF BEING OVERWHELMED BY THE PROBLEM

'QUALITY OF ATTENTION' SUCCESSFUL THERAPY

Towards the end of his life, Carl Rogers was asked what he felt was the most important element in the healing process. He replied that the key thing was the quality of attention the therapist gave to his client. This was more important than what the therapist said, or his qualifications, or the environment in which the therapy took place.

Rogers had observed that clients could tell when a therapist was genuinely interested in them and their well-being. If the therapist could create an atmosphere where clients felt totally safe and accepted – no matter what they might say or do – then Rogers believed they would be able to get to the root of their problems and eventually find solutions.

The requirements for the resolution of emotional problems include:

- empathetic listening
- reflective listening
- unconditional acceptance
- genuine attention

These are the things that Rogers encouraged in the therapists that he trained, and they form part of the wonderful legacy that he left, not only to the field of psychotherapy and counselling, but in the realm of human behaviour. All his work and his research led to a deeper understanding of the human condition.

BEING 'PERSON CENTRED'
HOW WE COULD LIVE OUR DAILY LIVES

Rogers was convinced that all human beings had locked deep within them the ability to reach their full potential. Empathetic listening and unconditional regard were the tools that would help unlock that potential.

More profoundly, Rogers believed that this approach to human beings – where people were fully heard and their views respected – was how people should be treated in day-to-day life by their parents, families and society at large. This empathetic approach should not just be reserved for the therapy room and the client/therapist relationship (which sadly was often the case). Rogers believed that in order for the world to attain peace, we had to begin by treating ourselves and each other in empathetic and unconditional ways that allowed individuals to be heard and understood. In this respect, Rogers was anti-totalitarian and against dogma and fundamentalism that crushed the individual under the weight of beliefs and ideas. In the end he, like Carl Jung before him, believed that the redemption of the entire human race would come about by individuals dealing with the fractured or damaged parts of their own souls – 'the shadow' as Jung called it – and not through mass movements or crusades which only led to more fractures in the form of totalitarianism and nationalism.

In this respect he shared Jung's fear that humanity would kill itself by not dealing first and foremost with the problems of individual conflict and pathology. While the Cold War threatened the world with the spectre of the mushroom cloud, Rogers dedicated his last years to spreading his gospel of listening.

ROGERS'S PLEA FOR WORLD PEACE

Rogers spent his last years travelling the world sharing his ideas on listening and conflict resolution with politicians and presidents on both sides of the Iron Curtain. It was partly his influence that helped to get people talking – and more importantly, listening – to each other. Cold War détente owed not a little to the culture of tolerance that Rogers encouraged in everyone he met.

Rogers was a latterday peacemaker of almost Biblical proportions, and in many people's eyes a sort of modern day saint. But he himself scrupulously avoided religiosity of any sort. It could be said that this was in reaction to his own strict religious upbringing. He rebelled against it all his life and would deliberately eschew any mention of 'spirituality' or 'God' in his work or in the process of inner healing. That was until the very end of his life, when he almost grudgingly accepted that something numinous and mysterious happened at the heart of the healing process; something akin to the gift of grace, where a mystical or transcendent force seemed to operate quietly to bring the healing to a sort of perfect completion that was beyond human wisdom.

Here we again find reference to our guiding spirit, the transcendent and mysterious force that visits man when he is at a loss or devastated; the force that seems to want to make the fracture knit again and bind the emotional wounds. And whatever we call it – be it our intuition or

KNOWING THE FOUNDATIONS OF YOUR HOUSE ARE FLAWED ALLOWS YOU TO TAKE CORRECTIVE ACTION. PRETENDING ALL IS WELL WILL NOT STOP THE HOUSE FROM FALLING DOWN!

our guardian angel, our conscience or the guiding spirit of our genius – really does not matter. What is important is allowing the 'force that binds' to work on the emotional wounds that need healing, in the same way that we encourage our body's own repair and immune system to knit broken bones and destroy viruses.

Later on we too will learn how to listen empathetically, as Carl Rogers taught it. By so doing, we will be touching that 'guiding awareness' inside, the part that helps us explore and find solutions to our most intimate problems.

6
—

EUGENE GENDLIN AND FOCUSING

If Carl Rogers discovered ways by which people could help
one another, namely empathetic listening and unconditional regard, Eugene Gendlin (a former student and
colleague of Rogers) went on to show how these methods
really worked. Rogers showed that something therapeutic
happened to a person's emotions when they were listened
to empathetically; Gendlin showed how and why.

He examined the internal mechanism for 'getting well',
taking it apart and explaining how it functioned. He found
that it was possible to get in touch with the psyche's
problem-solving process by following certain steps. These
steps enabled people immediately and directly to touch
this source of knowing. He called this process *Focusing*.

HEAD THINKING VERSUS GUT FEELING

Gendlin was able to identify how people could listen to
their bodies in a certain way. He discovered that there
were characteristic ways in which the body 'felt' or 'held'
a problem that were very different from the ways in which
it was viewed or 'thought about' in the head; and he found

that for true resolution to occur, it was necessary for the body to 'feel' the problem solved as well as 'thinking' it solved.

For example, let's listen to an 'everyday problem' of a client starting a Focusing session:

I had a row with a partner and we both left the house on bad terms – both blaming the other. But deep down inside my gut was a feeling that I was really rude to her – hurtfully so. This feeling was very insistent and kept on making me feel bad even though I didn't want to. I felt I should pick up the phone and apologise, but another part of me was too tired and dug in its heels and refused. So I returned home that night determined to act as if I had done nothing wrong – which a small part of me genuinely believed was true! But as I turned my key in the door I got a sinking feeling in the pit of my stomach that something was indeed badly wrong, and as it turned out my partner was very hurt and resentful at my behaviour. We had another blazing row and she walked out.

Later on I realised that I should have listened to that unsettling feeling in my body earlier and taken action. It's as if my body knew what my mind refused to accept. And however hard I tried to ignore it, it still kept warning me that something was wrong – that I really had to do something to save the day – but I didn't! And I regret that now. It's as if I failed to listen to my own 'early warning system'.

We have all had experiences like that, when we have known in our gut that our behaviour was wrong – but ego or selfishness or just plain laziness has prevailed and we have ignored the inner advice – usually to our regret.

LISTENING TO THE VOICE OF OUR CONSCIENCE

By learning to focus we will get a much clearer picture of what this inner voice is saying inside us – the insistent voice of conscience (or knowing). As a consequence we will be able to deal with inner conflict and emotional turmoil.

By learning to listen empathetically we will be able truly to hear what our loved ones, neighbours, work colleagues and families are saying to us. We will be able not only to listen but to feel what it is like to be in their shoes.

HAPHAZARD FOCUSING

Gendlin's research shows that we all focus in our lives to a greater or lesser extent. Focusing is a natural problem-solving process. (In fact artists and writers do something like it all the time.) What Gendlin discovered was this: when we focus without knowing it, we do it in a haphazard way. Being ignorant of the process, we have no idea what is actually happening, and when we do experience a focused solution to a problem, we have no real idea of how to replicate it. But once you know how to focus, you can do it any day – and every day.

Then you can apply it to almost any problem that

arises, from emotional problems and long-term self-esteem issues to finding solutions to a business plan or a novel, or working out how to write a dissertation or thesis. The creative possibilities are limitless.

THE SIX STEPS PROGRAMME

As Gendlin continued his research he was beginning to see what worked in therapy and what did not. The small percentage of people who succeeded in therapy all did one thing in common – they focused! They underwent a complex process which Gendlin eventually defined as involving six steps (although current research shows that the steps do not have to occur in their entirety or exact sequence for Focusing resolution to take place). He called these the 'Focusing steps'.

STEP 1

The clients are first able to get some 'distance' between themselves and the problem that has until now been 'overwhelming' them. They are able momentarily to 'stack' or place their problems to one side and feel once again what it was like to be 'problem free'.

STEP 2

The clients are then able to take these difficult feelings back inside themselves and get the bodily 'feel' of the problem once more. It stops being just an idea or a memory of the problem and becomes how they actually feel when the problem is present.

STEP 3

The clients then give this physical feeling of the problem their full attention – they begin to focus on it. And as they do so, a picture, word or image spontaneously comes to them after a few moments; an image that sums up exactly how the 'feeling' is experienced inside.

STEP 4

The client then checks this image or word back against the 'feeling' now felt in the body. Does it really describe it? After a moment a better word or image might come – one that absolutely fits the 'feeling'.

STEP 5

The client asks the feeling (now identified by the descriptive tag – the 'image' or 'word') two types of question. (It is important here to point out that the client is not addressing these questions to his intellect, his head, only, but to the holistic or whole body feel of the problem – the actual anxiety that he feels in his stomach and chest, the feeling for which he now has a real description.)

The first Focusing question looks to the past. The client asks the 'felt sense' (Gendlin's term for how the problem is felt in the body), 'What is the worst thing about all this?'

He then waits for an answer. He may wait a little time for the focus to sharpen, for the gut sense of the problem to open up and reveal itself. Certainly he will initially have to contend with the head firing off all the old pat answers that he is so used to. But if he has the patience to wait he will be rewarded with an answer that comes from deep within, like an intuition or inspiration. Something that is new and surprising, something he has not 'thought up' before.

It obviously requires something that knows what is actually going on in the unconscious if the problem is to be sorted out with any degree of satisfaction. And this is where Focusing strikes gold. For it goes right up to the coal-face of the unconscious, the place where the vague but uncomfortable feeling is felt, and asks it right there and then what is happening and what needs to be done. The place that knows what is 'wrong' is always *above* the place that knows what is 'right'! It's rather like looking under the bonnet of a car to find the cause of a worrying rattle. If you stop and lift the bonnet and look in while the engine is running, you will find not only the problem but also what needs to be done to rectify it. In other words the problem will also show you the solution.

In fact, if the Focusing process has worked, the client will be the most surprised person in the room. It will feel as if he has just been told something for the first time *by something or someone else inside him.* And this something changes his perception of the problem forever. At the end of the first question the client will be ready to move on to the second.

The second Focusing question unlocks the solution to the problem that is battering at the door of the client's unconscious. The client asks the unclear feeling of the problem: 'What needs to happen for this problem to be solved?'

Professor Gendlin found that when clients were able to ask this question and wait for the answer to come from within the problem, they experienced a profound resolution to what had previously appeared intractable – a problem that had defeated every attempt to solve it by head thinking.

It seems that when we give this sort of focused

attention to our problem feelings – when we allow them to be fully felt in our bodies and do not try to deny them or keep them as ideas in our heads – then something extraordinary happens: the problem itself seems to gives us the answer to our question.

Then we experience what Gendlin calls the 'felt shift' as the answer held in our body bursts through to consciousness. Now the focuser has a solution to the problem that is felt in the body. It is not just thought in the head. And with it comes an *action step* – something I can do practically to solve the problem.

The action step is the critical step in Focusing. It is what makes Focusing unique, for it goes beyond mere analysis to give the focuser a concrete step that will help to solve the particular problem. And as the answer comes from the individual with the problem it will fit uniquely in a way that no outside advice could.

STEP 6

The final step in Focusing is to thank the process for giving you a step forward, making sure that you:

- promise to visit this place again
- protect the Focusing insight from all the old conditioned responses that are waiting to knock it on the head!

This is vital if your new way of being is not going to be destroyed by old critical inner voices that say things like, 'This won't last!' or 'You don't think you'll be able to change things, do you?'

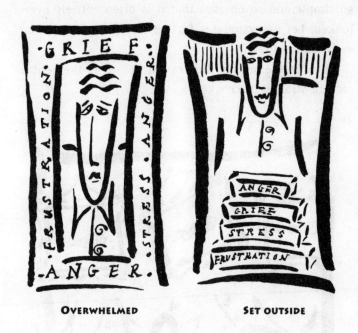

OVERWHELMED   **SET OUTSIDE**

WHY FOCUSING INSIGHTS WORK SO WELL

When we ask the Focusing questions we should expect
answers that are far more subtle and pointed than any
that can be worked out with mere intellect alone. For they
are coming from our own unconscious – the place that
knows all the intricate ins and outs of the problem and,
more importantly, all the unconscious forces that are
pushing us to do this or that. This is why solutions found
in Focusing always feel fresh and surprising.

*Focusing shows that in human beings the answer lies
behind the problem!*

This is the amazing paradox of Focusing. The point is so simple and so obvious that it is often entirely overlooked! Let us examine it further, for behind it lies an extraordinary reality.

Look at the simple illustration below. Is the centre picture straight or crooked?

Let us agree that it is crooked. Then ask yourself the following question: how do you know it is crooked? Take a moment to fill in the answer before you go on.

Q: How do I know the picture is crooked?

A: ....

The answer I am looking for is quite simple: I know the picture frame is crooked because I already have an idea of how it should be; I have an inner sense of what is 'straight' and I am comparing the picture to that inner knowing and finding it to be 'crooked'.

In fact, I can go one step further and say: I can only know the painting is crooked because I already know inside what is straight. Without knowing 'straightness' I cannot possibly know 'crookedness'. This knowledge is vital, for it allows me to take action and remedy the problem – I can now go up to the picture and 'straighten' it.

WHAT IS WRONG SHOWS US WHAT IS RIGHT!

This may sound obvious but it has profound implications when we come to apply it to the realm of human be-haviour. For here we find that the same thing applies, namely that human beings cannot know something is 'wrong' unless they first know what is right, or to be more exact, 'feel' what is right inside themselves.

Once we 'feel' something is wrong, it seems we have only to dig deep enough inside ourselves until we find what 'feels' right. Then we are only one step away from finding the remedy and being able to take action to 'right' the 'wrong' – just as we were able to take action and walk up and straighten the painting.

THE PROBLEM OF TRUSTING OURSELVES

The problem here, of course, is that our upbringing, both parental and educational, has so often left us feeling that answers are things that are 'learnt' from 'authorities', so we rarely have the confidence to look inside ourselves. In fact we often have no idea that there is an inside place we can look in!

That is why we inevitably turn to 'experts' - be they counsellors, therapists, teachers, priests or agony aunts - because we think they will have the answers.

BEING HUMBLE
'HOW COULD I POSSIBLY KNOW THE ANSWER?'

Furthermore, so many of us have been brought up being told that we could not possibly know the answer to anything because we:

- are too young
- are too stupid
- are too 'clever'
- are too 'bad'
- are the wrong 'class'
- have the wrong education
- are 'male' (or more likely 'female'!) or 'Irish' or 'Black'!

All these credentials can be thought to disbar you from knowing the answers when you are a young person. Once this attitude is learnt it is very difficult to get rid of and may stay to haunt you when you have grown to what is misguidedly called 'adult maturity'!

KNOWING 'RIGHT' FROM 'WRONG' – LITERALLY!

From all this comes one key conclusion: we can only know
something is *wrong* by first knowing what *right* feels like.
It is knowing how it should be and how it should feel that
alerts us to the fact that it no longer feels that way – it
no longer feels right in the body.

It seems that we have an inner sense of what 'feels'
right, a deep inner guide as to how it should feel or be
in our lives. Gendlin's research showed that this 'feeling'
is felt holistically in our bodies like a form of knowing
or 'conscience', and not as some idea thought up in the
head. In this respect, this sense of knowing that something is right in the body is very different from 'thinking'
something is right, in the head.

FOCUSING – THE CORE PROCESS OF
BECOMING EMOTIONALLY WELL

Research would suggest that Focusing is the core process
by which people become emotionally well and solve their
innermost problems. As such, knowing the tools of
Focusing can be profoundly helpful, giving people a
powerful method of dealing with their psychological
problems.

But Gendlin has always believed that Focusing should
not be reserved only for therapy. Fate or chance led to
its discovery coming from the therapeutic field, but that
does not mean that Focusing only works there. In fact,
as we have seen, it works in countless areas.

7
—

MY OWN EXPERIENCE
FOCUSING AND LISTENING
THE SECRET SKILL

I want to write about Focusing and share its power
because it has been such a wonderful addition to my life,
allowing me to learn how to listen and relate both to
myself and to others. What surprises me is how much of
a secret Focusing and listening skills are. I had a rounded
education, completing a degree in Art History before
pursuing a career in dance and choreography which
allowed me to work with people like Rudolf Nureyev,
Margot Fonteyn and the Kirov Ballet. But even coming
from an artistic (and supposedly enlightened!) background, I had never heard of things like client centred
therapy and empathetic listening.

LIVING 'FROM THE HEAD UP'

As a result I lived mainly 'from the head up', generally
experiencing life as I thought I should live it: through
concepts and ideas but not through feeling (except when
dancing or acting out a role – when we tend to focus

naturally). Otherwise I believed feelings were things to be distrusted – an attitude reinforced by a strict Jesuit upbringing.

In consequence I had wonderful career developments and transitions but lousy relationships, no doubt due to my inability to understand my own cut-off feelings. It took me several years of unsuccessful therapy and several disappointing relationships before I came across Focusing and listening.

MY OWN INTRODUCTION TO FOCUSING

For several weeks I had been distraught. It was just before Christmas and I had only recently broken up with someone who had been very close to me. For me it did not feel like the end of a relationship – it felt like the end of the world! I was encountering frightening feelings that I had experienced many times before when other relationships had ended. I had undergone therapy in order to prevent such a recurrence and I thought that I had gone some way to solving the problem, but here I was again with a feeling of dread in the pit of my stomach and a constant anxiety occupying my mind as I alternately thought about my ex-partner then tried to push any thoughts of her out of my head.

But they stubbornly refused to go; or if they did it was only for a short while before they returned and threatened to overwhelm me. It was then that I heard the old familiar voice in my mind shouting me down: 'Why didn't you do this?' or 'I told you not to do that!' – either berating me for my behaviour towards her or planning some new strategy to get her back; and there was no escape from it. The downward spiral continued with my becoming even more depressed the more my efforts to control my thoughts and feelings failed.

THE ADVICE OF FRIENDS

I sought the advice of friends who were as helpful as they could be – 'Don't worry, it was not meant to be,' they said, or 'Everything will be fine – just put it out of your head!' I listened to my friends and tried to follow their advice. When a friend said, 'Be strong, there is no need for this depression – you'll end up in an early grave!' I would try desperately to be strong the next day, coaxing and cajoling myself into feeling strong and positive, making an effort to go out and meet new people. But although I tried hard I knew my heart wasn't in it. In the end I just felt empty. It was as if there was something wrong inside; something that I could feel but not put my finger on – something that did not respond to my efforts to *act* in the way my friends suggested. Also I realised that I could not put the memory of the old relationship out of my mind and I knew that the pain of absence was actually getting worse.

DAILY LIFE DISRUPTED

I was not able to eat properly and my sleep was affected. I'd wake up every morning and for a moment I'd feel fine, then the memories of my partner would start flooding back and the lead weight of depression would settle once more in the pit of my stomach; a weight that would remain there for the rest of the day, despite all my efforts to get rid of it.

Soon my feelings of failure and disappointment began to affect every area of my life. My ability to concentrate on work was disrupted. I would begin a task but the thoughts would start creeping back in and work became difficult if not impossible to complete as my mind brooded.

Sometimes my resolve to keep away from my ex-partner would waver. Much of my time was occupied in a pointless debate as to whether I should phone her or not. I was fast getting into an obsessive state and, try as I might, I did not seem to be able to dig myself out of it. I was beginning to get worried.

SYMPTOM OF EMOTIONAL PAIN

The main physical symptom of all this turmoil was a ball of pain in the pit of my stomach. It would not go away whatever I did. I had tried counselling over the years but that did not seem to work. I had tried to talk it out with my friends – a number of whom were counsellors and therapists – but this did not seem to make it better.

I went back on the cigarettes – smoking twenty-plus a day, using them to get temporary relief from the dull, aching pain inside. But my inability to make things better was worrying me. It was, after all, only a broken heart I was suffering from. Why could I not control or blot out the destructive and damaging feelings that were eating away at my insides – feelings that were threatening to overwhelm me and lead to a breakdown if I was not careful?

COUNSELLING

Over the years I had certainly tried to understand and control my feelings. I had gone through counselling and reached a certain insight as to why I was acting and feeling the way I did – but that knowledge did not help me get rid of my feelings.

I applied 'positive thinking' strategies to my problem, studying Neuro-linguistic Programming (NLP) and other techniques for improving my state of mind. These worked initially but after a day or two the relief would wear off, or something would come along that reminded me of my ex-partner and the old wounds would open up again. I taught positive visualisation as part of my stress management work and now I tried to imagine my pain and emotional difficulties disappearing from my life. It worked for a while but soon the same old nagging pain was back.

DECISION TIME

One night I was sitting in a bar in a dreadful state of anxiety bordering on despair. Suddenly I felt a surge of anger at myself for my weakness and the way in which I was allowing my life to become so dark and depressed. On an instinct I finished my drink and went outside to walk. As I walked along I decided that I would concentrate with absolute belief and will-power to obliterate the dark feelings that were in my heart and replace them with positive thoughts. I can remember taking a deep breath and concentrating my mind totally as I purged it once and for all of every depressive thought. 'Get out and stay out!' I shouted as I willed the change with every atom of my body. 'You will not overcome me!'

I don't think I have ever willed anything so strongly; I was convinced I could change the structure of my mind by sheer will-power. I put everything into it and did not even consider the possibility that it might fail; my mind was too intent on getting rid of the pain. I believed that if I concentrated on eliminating the feelings during every waking moment of my day, they would not have a chance to come back and haunt me.

I went home and slept, feeling that I was back in charge of things and that I had turned a corner.

THE POWERLESSNESS OF POSITIVE THINKING

How little I really understood myself! I awoke the next morning and within minutes the dark feelings were back. I again tried to get rid of them and managed to keep it up for a few hours until I collapsed exhausted under the weight of the effort. It was not working. I had discovered that I could not control every painful thought and feeling that I experienced, no matter how positive I was or how much faith I put into it. I had come to realise that there was another reality, one that existed outside my will but inside my body, where there were strong feelings that would not be bullied about.

But for now I was exhausted. I had tried prayer,

therapy, positive thinking, visualisation, talking it out, denying that I felt bad at all, getting busy so that I would not notice it, numbing it with cigarettes, and taking the counsel and advice of friends and 'experts'. I had read and listened to every 'self-help' book and tape I could get my hands on, but rather than receding, the dark and depressed feelings were getting worse and I had no idea what to do next.

SERENDIPITY – A RAY OF HOPE

It was then that serendipity stepped in. I was recommended to someone who did 'Focusing', some new therapy from America that I had never heard of. I decided to go along and give it a go. I had nothing to lose.

BEING LISTENED TO FOR THE FIRST TIME

I can remember the first meeting quite clearly. My teacher for the session was a very accomplished and experienced Focusing guide who had come across Focusing while studying in America. I sat in her room and she began by asking me how she could help. I started to explain my predicament to her. I remember that I was expecting her to give me some good advice based on her wisdom. But she did not. Instead she did something that I had not experienced before – she listened to me with total concentration and without interrupting me to give her advice or opinion.

This was quite a disturbing experience, for it allowed me, as I explained my position to her, to see just how confused and upset I really was. Usually when I was explaining my upset to someone they would rush in with words of comfort or advice and I never got very far in my story. Perhaps they were too uncomfortable to hear how upset I was. Anyway, hearing myself speak for thirty minutes without being interrupted and told what to feel, was difficult but enlightening.

SEEING MY OWN CONFUSION

I can remember sitting there describing all my fears and complexes and thinking, as she gently repeated them back to me, what an idiot she must have thought I was - for it all sounded ridiculously complicated and contradictory as I heard myself describe it.

'This really is a mess!' I remember thinking as I saw it all mixed up like a giant ball of tangled wool. It was only later, when I was studying listening and Focusing, that I understood what she had done, and the gentle and profound skill it required. But as I recall that first session, I am struck by the impact it had on me. I truly saw my own pain and confusion for the first time with my own eyes.

ASKING ADVICE - SEEKING APPROVAL

After I had spoken and described as best I could the emotional hurricane that was raging through my body, I sat and looked at her, waiting for the sort of judgement I was used to receiving - 'How terrible of her!' - or sympathy - 'You must feel devastated!' - followed by the inevitable advice – 'You should forget about her!' – all the things I had heard over the last few weeks. But this time it was different. This time nothing happened. No advice was given; no judgement was passed. We just sat for a moment in silence. Eventually I asked the question that had been bubbling up in my chest for some time – the question we are all programmed to ask. I asked her what she thought and what I should do next. I wanted her to assume responsibility for any action I might take. Luckily for me, she did not do so. Instead she invited me to focus on the problem. Little did I know it then, but this was the start of a long process to repair a damaged heart.

THE VALUE OF TRUE LISTENING

My guide showed an expert's knowledge as she listened and quietly repeated back to me the words I had just said in a way that was so subtle I did not even notice. As a result I began to form a picture in my own mind of the true state I was in. That first 'listening' session went like this.

Kevin: I feel very bad about the way it ended. I feel I let her down badly ... and I want to make it up to her, but that's not possible now ... (silent and upset)

Facilitator: So you feel bad about it, but don't think it's possible to make it up with her.

Kevin: (pause as he reflects on this) No, I don't – but it's more than that ... it's like I'm afraid to do it now. (pause) I'm terrified she'll reject me again ...

Facilitator: So that's how it is, it's not just that you can't go back to her, it's more like you're afraid of her because you fear she'll reject you again.

Kevin: (reflects before replying) Yes! I'm afraid and I sense that she knows I'm afraid . . . and that makes her want me even less – she doesn't want someone who's spineless. I feel panicky about that – her not wanting me . . . I'm afraid of what will happen now. I feel I will curl up and die if she doesn't come back to me but that's what I'm afraid will happen. I feel real panicky . . .

Facilitator: So that's how it feels for you – a sense of real panic.

Kevin: (pause and tears begin to fall) Yes, but even though I know that it wasn't working out . . . (difficulty speaking) I still miss her terribly . . . but she won't come back now . . . that is what I fear the most . . . it's a real mess . . .

Facilitator: You fear that she will not come back.

Kevin: (breathing disrupted by sobs) Yes, and I don't think I can take that . . . I don't think I can survive that . . .

Facilitator: That's something you don't feel you can survive.

Kevin: Yes . . . and you know that worries me.

As I heard back all that was going on in my life, it was as if I could see it from a different point of view, from outside myself. I could see my life as it was and not how I would like it to be; and because we didn't get involved in what she thought of my situation, I was able to get an image of myself *by myself*. This was a profound and useful experience that gave me some relief from the overwhelming feelings I had been experiencing.

I Begin to 'Focus' on the Problem

Once I had found some space between myself and the feelings, the facilitator moved on and helped me 'focus' on them. She began by asking me how I felt.

> *Kevin*: (sigh) It feels like my whole life is just one great ball of confusion – it's like a giant ball of wool.
> *Facilitator*: Can you stay with that 'ball of confusion'? Is it possible just to be with it?
> *Kevin*: (pause) Yes, I can see it up there in front of me! It's huge! It's like a huge ball of wool. But the strands of the ball are not made out of wool, they're made out of steel and they are hard. It's total confusion in there! (laughs sadly) Hard and confusing – I just can't see through it at all! It's like it covers everything – it's so big . . .

At this point it is important to point out what Carl Jung discovered. He found that the psyche spoke most naturally in 'images' rather than 'words', as in dreaming. In fact some commentators have remarked that Focusing is like 'wide-awake dreaming'.

As I began my first Focusing session, this is exactly what was starting to happen to me. The 'ball of wool' was the 'image' of how I was feeling. My psyche had been encouraged to express itself in this way by the listening process.

The facilitator then asked if it was possible for me to give this 'hard and confusing' feeling my attention. She suggested that it might help to close my eyes if I felt comfortable doing so. I closed my eyes and brought my attention to the place in my body she suggested – the area between the pit of my stomach and my Adam's apple.

At first it was a very difficult thing to do. I kept jumping up into my head which kept on firing ideas at me and I was not sure if I was merely imagining being down there in my body while still staying up in the head. I was so used to being in my head and thinking from my head that it seemed rather absurd to be concentrating 'down there' in my gut. How could that possibly help?

At first I could hardly make sense of her request. But slowly things began to happen as she got me to notice what it felt like down there in the centre of my body. In the end I stopped analysing for long enough to notice what it really felt like in my body. I began to notice great pain down there in my stomach; pain and a tension that I had never noticed before. I got a sudden bodily intuition that if I kept on being stressed like this I would get seriously ill; my body could not survive the strain. It was an amazingly powerful sensation, and quite disturbing, as I began to feel the damage I was doing myself, realising that my body as well as my head carried 'feelings'. It was as if my body were talking to me!

THE FOCUSING IMAGE – FEELINGS TAKE SHAPE

Then something extraordinary happened. As I kept focusing on my body I saw something begin to take shape inside my chest. It was like a giant cable – the sort that is laid at the bottom of the ocean; but it was so thick that it resembled the trunk of a huge tree that had been twisted around on itself, like a piece of washing that had been wrung out. I looked at this huge object that now occupied the core of my being, reaching up from the depths of my stomach, and marvelled at it in a horrified kind of way.

I was not quite sure what it was but my Focusing guide merely asked me if it was possible to give it my attention and get a feel of it without trying to analyse it or get rid of it or go back into my head. With an effort I brought my attention back to my body and resumed looking at the huge black cable that lay coiled like some great serpent in the middle of my body. And as I looked at it I felt a strange sense that it badly needed my attention.

GIVING THE IMAGE SOME ATTENTION

I was not afraid of it; it was more that I was struck by its actual presence there in the middle of my body, for I knew I had not made it appear there myself, as by an effort of imagination. And with this bodily felt image came a sense of surprise and curiosity and then a deep sadness. But it was a sadness mixed with awe at what was happening. It was like going around a funfair and not knowing what strange and terrifying ride was coming next. And above all was an excitement at the realisation that I was not making this whole thing up in my head.

THE MYSTERIOUS RELIEF

I stayed with the image and the sadness for quite some time, just giving it attention. It was then that I began to cry, realising that my life was somehow overshadowed by a mysterious and unaccountable grief; a grief that was strangely tortured and twisted out of shape – just like this image. But oddly for me, with that realisation came a great sense of relief. It was as if realising that I was filled with some terrible inward pain, and admitting it, made it feel so much better.

ACKNOWLEDGING THE MYSTERIOUS SADNESS

The sadness had not gone away, nor did I understand it any better – but knowing it was there in this way sent a flood of relief through my body. It's like finding out from the doctor that you are actually ill, and not merely imagining it. You can stop worrying and go and sort it out. That is the nearest to how I felt just then. The tears were good tears and for the first time in months I felt light inside. I was still 'ill' but at least I had a sense of deep, heartfelt relief (for however short a time) and a sense that something extraordinary had just happened.

We finished that first session and made the next appointment and I left feeling elated and shaken. For a long time after, I reflected on my first encounter with Focusing. I had never come across anything quite like it and nothing had prepared me for it. It was not that the Focusing feeling felt in any way 'better' than other experiences I had had in my life – it was just that I was gobsmacked that I could feel such extraordinary emotions. It was the entirely different quality and nature of the feeling that struck me. Primarily it was the sense of being talked to inside by something that was not infected by my own fears and conditioning. It was like being 'enlightened'.

I have described in detail my first Focusing session in the hope that it will give you some idea of how Focusing and empathetic listening really work first-hand. Now we can go on to learn how to focus ourselves.

PART 2

LEARNING TO FOCUS

8

How Can I Experience Focusing?

Focusing is something you *do* rather than *think* or *talk* about. It is an 'experience' and the best way to understand it is to experience it. So let us gently start to focus!

Focusing is about becoming more aware, and there are many ways in which we can do this. The whole object of the exercise is slowly to get out of 'head thinking' and into 'body feeling'. It is quite simple to describe. Remember: there is no *right* way to do these exercises. All you need to do is your best – the rest will follow.

SERENDIPITY

Serendipity is when good fortune favours you in a special way. For example: you have been looking to call an old friend but have lost his phone number and have no means of getting it again. The next day you are walking down the street when you suddenly bump into that person head-on. It's a great feeling – you feel as if the world is somehow looking after you.

Well it is! Research into serendipity and its sister 'synchronicity' (when time or coincidence work to your

82

favour) shows that all the time we are being gifted with opportunities to make up for lost time and human mistakes. We have only to keep our eyes open and sharpen our awareness just a little to see how the universe is working to our betterment. Picking up a book or being given one as a gift is often part of this universal serendipity.

Begin to read these pages, start to do these Focusing exercises and something will start to happen inside you and in your life. You will be corresponding with the power in the universe that wants you to become more aware – and it will repay your interest and energy in due measure and help you.

ALL YOU HAVE TO DO IS TRY!

Simply trying is enough. You don't have to 'get it right', any more than you try to 'get right' walking to work or feeding the ducks in the park! As long as you do your best, that will be enough.

GETTING READY FOR THE EXERCISE

Notice the chair you are sitting on right *now!* Soon we will notice several areas of your body and how they feel. Take your time. You can take fifteen seconds or fifteen minutes to focus on each part of your body – you decide the time. If your mind wanders or you get bored, that's all right. Simply bring it gently back or move on to the next body part. And remember – you can finish whenever you like. Start relying on your body to tell you when you have had enough.

Remember: there are *no* Brownie points for labouring through this or any other exercise to the bitter end. Focusing is all about increasing your awareness and not suffering in silence. Focusing awareness is our goal. When your awareness begins to dim or wander, notice it and gently try to re-focus. If this does not work, simply ask your body if it needs to take a rest.

N. B. It may be a good idea to switch off the phone and tell people you do not want to be disturbed for a few minutes. It is very frustrating to be interrupted in the middle of a session.

9
—

FOCUSING EXERCISE 1
GETTING OUT OF MY 'HEAD THINKING'

WE ARE MORE THAN OUR THOUGHTS

We go on existing when we cease thinking, and so we can safely assume that we are more than our thoughts. So what happens when we stop thinking? There is only one way to find out – let's try it!

This first exercise helps us see that we are more than just our thoughts.

THE SPACE BETWEEN OUR THOUGHTS

I would like you to notice what happens when you stop thinking. This should not be too difficult. You probably got a lot of practice at school! Simply finish this paragraph and let your eyes rest on the blank space below. You do not have to think of anything at all – simply see what happens when you momentarily stop thinking. See what happens in the *space between your thoughts*.

Notice anything? Notice how things go quiet but you sense that there is something still there? Try it again. Just stare at the blank space under this for about twenty seconds without thinking of anything in particular, just let your mind idle . . .

Notice something? A presence – a sort of 'knowing'? Try it again . . . Can you feel it? Can you sense it? You can go back to it at any time you choose.

It's strange, but in the space between our thoughts we find that something is there – we are not alone! It's like a presence . . . a Silent Watcher who fills the space between my thoughts. Try it again and see . . . It's always there, a presence that seems to occupy the background of our minds. A palpable awareness that is as real as it is ever-present. It feels 'a part of me' and 'apart from me' – both at the same time!

JUNG AND HIS 'WISE OLD MAN'

Carl Jung encountered a startling presence in one of his dreams and he called it his 'Wise Old Man'. In the dream the old man, complete with white beard and long coat, came and warned Jung about certain events.

86

This figure of the 'Wise Old Man' could be seen as another aspect of the Silent Watcher, who whispers to us, both while we wake and while we sleep, giving us insights, dreams and inspirations. It tends to communicate to us not just through words but through 'feelings'. It's as if we 'feel' what it is telling us, and this 'feeling' is felt somewhere inside our minds and our bodies. Try it again: linger for several seconds in the space between your thoughts and notice how you 'feel' (rather than what you 'hear'). Can you sense the presence of something or someone there? A wisdom or ancient knowing?

Try it and see . . .

'FEELING' THE SILENT WATCHER INSIDE

Indeed, the sense of what the Watcher is saying is often 'felt' in our gut, rather than 'heard' in our head. It is the sort of knowing that is visceral rather than cerebral. People often experience this sort of sensation when they get a 'gut feeling' about something. And as we all know, gut feelings are often right!

But go by your own instinct. Everyone experiences this differently. As I rest in the space between my thoughts right now, I notice a lively, probing energy inside. It has a life of its own; and after a moment I notice that it is silently analysing and commenting on what I am writing, giving me a 'feeling' as to the quality of the work and a sense of where I should go from here. It also gives me an unsettled feeling in the stomach when it feels I have got a point wrong!

'Feeling' as Information

This 'feeling' is for me and a part of me but it is not the whole of me, and in some ways I feel it is outside of me; particularly in the sense that I cannot control it or shut it up when it warns me that I am doing something wrong.

For it often goes against my wishes and desires and furthermore it demands that I take action that will cost me dear in time, energy and sacrifice. There are things I may not want to do right now, like confront someone in my family or take on a lazy work colleague; and it won't go away when I get angry with it or when I ignore it, pretend it is not there and omit to take corrective action. It keeps at me till I take some sort of notice of it – even if that is only to dismiss it. But then I had better watch out – for if I dismiss it, it will go on to make my life a misery!

The Voice of Conscience

In many ways this 'wise old presence' is the voice of *conscience*. This is the one voice that will not shut up, however hard you try to make it do so. You can kill it – and many do (how else would the killing factories in Auschwitz and in Bosnia exist?) – but you will do so at a terrible cost. Many psychiatrists now believe that failing to listen to this voice can ultimately lead to depression and illness – both mental and physical; and the reason for this is simple.

It seems that this voice of conscience, the voice of the 'ancient wisdom', actually knows what is right for me. It is just that sometimes I do not have the inner courage to follow it.

WHAT IS CONSCIENCE?

The word 'conscience' is derived from two Latin words: *con-* meaning 'together' and *scire*, the verb 'to know', or 'to be with knowing'.

The word has come to encompass several subtle variations of meaning, from 'the exercise of judgement on moral questions' to 'an infallible guide to human behaviour' or a sort of 'guiding deity within' (notice how close this is to the Roman definition of *genius* as the 'guiding spirit within').

Conscience consists of an inner certainty or knowing. It is experienced by us especially at times of trial, when we are faced with difficult decisions and are inclined to make a choice that in the short term looks more attractive but in the long term may have graver consequences. Conscience also appears when we are faced with decisions that require moral courage and self-sacrifice.

CONSCIENCE AS THE GUIDING VOICE WITHIN

Perhaps we can conclude that conscience is the guiding spirit at work. It certainly seems to talk to us from somewhere outside ourselves and our ego – which can be selfish and blinkered in its pursuit of gratification.

The other remarkable thing about conscience is how it is 'felt' not in the head or as a cerebral idea, but rather in the heart and the gut.

It is difficult to argue your way around conscience, justifying the unjustifiable; and you can never rid yourself of the physical discomfort felt in the pit of your stomach when you 'know' you are doing something wrong or omitting to do something you should. In this sense conscience is an infallible guide. It cannot be bought, sold or compromised.

Tips

Take it easy at first. Don't try to make the exercise work. It will come with time and practice. Practise these exercises as often as you like – they will help you to become aware of the voice of your inner wisdom.

10

FOCUSING EXERCISE 2
BRINGING AWARENESS INTO THE BODY

This exercise is about bringing your awareness into your body at a very fundamental level. We know from Gendlin's research that the body is a vital source of information; especially emotional information. It is like a large tuning fork, vibrating with inner emotion. The best way of accessing this information is to tune into the body itself and begin listening to it. And one of the best ways to start this is to notice first exactly how much space your body takes up.

This is also useful as it starts to get you out of your head. But some people are so used to living in their heads that it is very difficult for them even to get a sense that they have a body. This exercise will help you get a sense of the rest of your body. It will also help to ground you, giving you a sense of the earth on which you walk and live. Only consider the questions for as long as you like. Try not to answer them in your head – rather wait and see what comes to you spontaneously as a visceral 'gut' or body feeling.

If a question doesn't make sense, move on.

START OF EXERCISE 2
LET ME BECOME AWARE OF . . .

MY FEET

You have tiny receptors in your feet that tell you exactly how much space your feet are taking up at any given moment. You can usually make yourself aware of this by noticing your feet pressing against the inner lining of your shoes or socks.

- How big do your feet feel?
- What part of them is resting on the floor?
- Just bring your attention gently down towards your feet and see if you can get some definite sensory feedback or awareness of how much space they are occupying right now.

When you have decided that you have spent enough time with one particular part of your body, move on.

LEGS

Using the same approach, try bringing your attention down to your legs.

- Focus in on the space between your ankles and your hip bone and, using the same receptors, see if you can get a sense of how much space your legs take up in the room right now.
- See if you can get a sense of the shape of your lower leg and then your knee joint and upper leg.
- How big are your thighs?

Remember you *don't* have to get this exercise 'right' – just trying is enough to increase your awareness.

STOMACH

Now bring your attention to the area between the base of your spine and the top of your stomach.

- How much space does this part of your body take up?
- Can you get a sense of how cylindrical your stomach is?
- How it presses against your belt or trousers?
- And how much space is inside it?

When you have finished, move on in your own time.

CHEST

Now bring your attention to the place between the top of your tummy and your throat.

- Notice how much space your chest occupies in the room right now.
- Notice how much space it occupies when you breathe in and when you breathe out – can you feel the difference?
- Stay with this for as long as you like, noticing how your chest rises and falls as you breathe.
- How much space does the air in your lungs take up?

Move on when you feel ready.

SHOULDERS AND NECK

- Take a moment to notice how much space your neck and shoulders take up.
- You can move your neck gently from side to side or

stretch your shoulders just to get a sense of how much space they occupy.

- Are the shoulders rounded or sloped?
- Is the space your shoulder occupies compressed or tight?
- Check for yourself and change your posture if it feels more comfortable to do so.

Move on when you are ready.

ARMS AND HANDS

Now check the space between your shoulder socket and your fingertips.

- How much space do your upper arms take up?
- Your lower arms and wrists?
- Your palms and fingers?
- Your fingertips?

When you have a sense of this move on.

MOUTH AND TONGUE

- How much space does your mouth take up, and your tongue?
- Move your tongue around and stretch your jaw from side to side.
- Swallow and notice how the saliva goes down into your tummy.
- Notice what taste you have in your mouth right now.
- When did you last really relish a meal?
- How important is taste in your life?

Move on when you are ready.

Nose

- Notice how much space your nose takes up.
- What is its shape?
- How does the air feel when you breathe it in?
- How does the air feel when you breathe it out?
- When did you last smell something that gave you pleasure?
- How important is your sense of smell?

Move on when you are ready.

Ears

- How much space do your ears take up?
- What sounds can you hear right now?
- In your body and head?
- In the room?
- Outside the room?
- When did you last hear sounds that pleased you?
- Voices that pleased you?
- How important is sound in your life?

Move on when you are ready.

Eyes

- How much space do your eyes and eyelids take up?
- What can you see right now in front of you? How does this page look?
- What can you see around you?
- What colours?
- What textures?
- How important is sight to you?

Move on when you are ready.

HEAD

- How much space does your head take up right now?
- And your brain?
- Can you feel your head working right now so that you can read this question?
- What are you conscious of right now?
- Can you notice the gaps between your thoughts?
- What happens in the gaps between your thoughts?
- What's it like to be *you*?

Move on when you are ready.

FINALLY

- Can you sense your body working and informing you right now?
- Is your body right now trying to tell you something?
- If so, can you take a moment to rest in silence and listen?
- Does anything come, something you might like to write down?
- Finally take a moment to check how you are feeling right now – all over your body and inside of it.
- Do you feel the same as when you started the exercise?
- If not, where is the difference felt?

Remember: you do not have to answer this or any other question! Especially with your head. Just let it settle in the middle of your body and see what comes. You may get a whisper or an insight or a sudden intuition. And you may get nothing at all. It does not really matter; all that matters is that you are asking – and we are told that those who ask receive!

How Often Should I Do the Second Exercise?

As often as you like. You can do this exercise throughout life as a way of finding your own space. If this is your first time at this sort of thing, do the exercise several times until you get comfortable doing it, before moving on to the next.

Try it with a friend. You read it out to them while they do it and vice versa. This way you get to experience both guiding someone and doing the exercise.

Remember: this is not a test or exam. You are doing the exercise to increase your awareness of your body.

11

FOCUSING EXERCISE 3
HOW THE BODY FEELS

In the last exercise we were looking for a sense of being aware of the body's own space, as the first step in listening to the body in a focused way. In the next exercise we will begin to listen to how the body feels.

It starts off just like the second exercise but builds on it, inviting you to become aware of how the body feels in its tissues – tissues that vibrate with feeling at a deep level.

When you first do this exercise you will perhaps find it hard to get this sense of 'feeling'. But stay with it – it is there. It just takes a little time to discover. Once you do you will be opening a door into the rich vein of feeling that provides the raw material for Focusing.

Find a comfortable, quiet place and take the phone off the hook. Now we are ready to begin our session.

98

START OF EXERCISE 3
BODY PARTS TO BECOME AWARE OF

FEET

- Just bring your attention gently down towards your feet and see if you can get some definite sensory feedback or awareness of how much space they take up right now.
- When you have got a sense of that, keep your attention there and notice how your feet feel right now.

They may feel one of many sensations ranging from heavy to tired to light. Or they may feel a mixture of feelings or nothing at all. But remember – numbness or absence of feeling *is a feeling as well!* – and you can notice and work with that.

Your goal here is simply to notice how your body feels right now. You do not have to make anything up or get the exercise 'right'. You are simply noticing what is already there in your body and how it is carrying your emotional feelings. Once you have done that the process will do the rest for you – you do not have to do anything!

When you have decided that you have spent enough time with one particular part of your body, move on.

LEGS

Using the same approach, try bringing your attention down to your legs.

- Focus in on the space between your ankles and your hip bone and, using the same receptors, see if you can get a sense of how much space your legs take up in the room right now.

- Now when you have spent enough time getting a sense of how much space your legs occupy, notice how they feel right now.
- Do they feel light, heavy, large, small, stretched, tired, limitless or sad? What word comes to you?

Remember: these exercises do not have to make sense right away. Just keep bringing your attention to your body in this way and see what happens.When you have spent enough time move on.

STOMACH

Now bring your attention to the area between the base of your spine and the top of your stomach.

- How much space does this part of your body take up?
- Can you get a sense of how cylindrical your stomach is?
- How it presses against your belt or trousers?
- And how much space is inside of it?
- Now see if you can get a sense of how this part of your body feels.

Your stomach is one of the most sensitive parts of the body as regards emotional feeling. It registers happiness, anxiety and sadness. Visceral or gut feeling is an important indicator of how you really feel about people and life events. The stomach is also the area of the body that is flooded by the 'fight or flight' hormones like adrenaline and cortisol. That is why we get anxious 'butterflies in the tummy' feelings when we are stressed.

- What is your feeling in the pit of your stomach right now?

Do not answer straight away from your head with a 'What's he talking about?' or 'I feel nothing!' response. Gendlin found that it can take thirty seconds for the attention to come down from the head to the gut and get a visceral response.

And remember, there may well be more than one emotion; there may be a mixture of many. And you will begin to identify them as you become familiar with this exercise.

When you have finished, move on in your own time.

CHEST

Now bring your attention to the place between the top of your tummy and your throat.

- Notice how much space your chest occupies in the room right now.
- Notice how much space it occupies when you breathe in and when you breathe out – can you feel the difference?

Your breathing is a very accurate barometer of feeling. When people are frightened or anxious their breathing immediately reflects this. When you are tired you yawn, when happy you laugh and when sexually aroused you sigh, breathe deeply and moan! Breathing is literally 'the Breath of Life', as the Zen Buddhists say.

- How is your breathing right now and how does it feel?

Move on when you feel ready.

- Take a moment to notice how much space your neck and shoulders take up. You can move your neck gently from side to side or stretch your shoulders just to get a sense of how much space they occupy.

The shoulders are the place where we literally and metaphorically carry our burdens in life and our stress. Go into town and look around at people. It will not take long to see people with slumped shoulders who are literally 'weighed down by life'!

- How do your shoulders and neck feel?
- What burdens – if any – are they carrying?

Stay at least thirty seconds with each part to discover how it really 'feels' before moving on. Change your posture if it feels more comfortable to do so.

Now check the space between your shoulder socket and your fingertips.

- How much space do your upper arms take up?
- Your lower arms and wrists?
- Your palms and fingers?
- Your fingertips?
- Now how do your arms and hands feel?

When you have a sense of this move on.

MOUTH AND TONGUE

- How much space does your mouth take up, and your tongue?
- Move your tongue around and stretch your jaw from side to side.
- Swallow and notice how the saliva goes down into your tummy.
- How important is taste in your life?
- Notice how this part of your body feels.

Move on when you are ready.

NOSE

- Notice how much space your nose takes up.
- What is its shape?
- How does the air feel when you breathe it in?
- How does the air feel when you breathe it out?
- How does this part of your body feel?

Move on when you are ready.

EARS

- How much space do your ears take up?
- What sounds can you hear right now?
- In your body and head?
- In the room?
- Outside of the room?
- When did you last hear voices that pleased you?
- How do your ears feel right now?

We often feel tired of listening to people moaning and complaining – and this can include ourselves!

- Notice if your sense of hearing is affected by everything it is exposed to all day and night.
- How does it 'feel' about life?

Move on when you are ready.

EYES

- How much space do your eyes and eyelids take up?
- What can you see right now in front of you? How does this page look?
- What can you see around you?
- What colours?
- What textures?
- How important is sight to you?

Like our sense of smell, our eyes are affected by all that they see each day. Leonardo da Vinci called them 'the windows of the soul'.

- How do your eyes 'feel' right now?
- Are they sick of what they see or delighted? Take a moment to find out.

Move on when you are ready.

HEAD

- How much space does your head take up right now?
- And your brain?
- Can you feel your head working right now so that you can read this question?
- What are you conscious of right now?

In coming to the head we come to a place where a lot goes

on. It is the brain that receives all the stimuli. It is here that stress and anxiety are created. This is the part that decides what is OK in life and what is terrifying. It is one of the most complex organisms yet discovered in the universe.

- Can you sense your brain working and informing you right now?
- How does it feel?
- Is it trying to tell you something?
- If so, can you take a moment to rest in silence and listen?
- Does anything come, something you might like to write down?

Only consider these questions for as long as you like. Try not to answer them with your head – rather wait and see what comes to you spontaneously in your body.

FINALLY

- Take a moment to check how you are feeling right now – all over your body and inside of it.
- Do you feel the same as when you started the exercise?
- If not, where is the difference felt?
- Finally, as you sit there, just let the following question form in your mind: what does it 'feel' like being aware of 'me' right now?

When you have finished, take all the time you need to come back. It may feel right to thank the body for all that it has shown you; and you may want to tell it that you will come back to it soon.

DURATION OF EXERCISE

Let your body tell you how long it needs to spend with each complete exercise. As a guideline, it should not be less than five to ten minutes. There is no upper limit, but if it goes over half an hour your attention and awareness may drift. When you feel your awareness slipping, that is the time either to move on or to stop.

12

FOCUSING EXERCISE 4
WHAT ARE THE 'ISSUES IN MY TISSUES'?

Now we are moving into Focusing proper and beginning
to identify the issues that your body is carrying – perhaps
without your fully realising it.

Do not attempt this exercise until you have spent a
couple of weeks doing the first three Focusing exercises
and the first two listening exercises.

These will give you a real sense of being aware of your
body and how it is feeling. Once you can identify how the
body is feeling, then you can begin to focus on the 'issues
in your tissues'!

START OF EXERCISE 4: BODY AWARENESS

Become aware of what is supporting your:

- feet
- buttocks
- back
- neck and shoulders
- arms and hands

When you have a sense of this, focus your attention on what feels for you like the centre or core of your body, the place where you feel things are really going on inside. Notice how it feels down there. Then ask the centre of your body the following central question:

• Is there anything in my life that's getting in the way of my feeling really good right now?

Don't answer right away. Take time to answer this question. Remember your head will fire off lots of quick problems. But these are not necessarily what you are looking for right now. Anyway, you know these *head problems*; you are dealing with them every day. What you are looking for is the visceral or gut-felt problem that the head may not be consciously aware of right now because it is too preoccupied or busy. The problem may be too awkward or painful for your mind to deal with right now. In fact your mind may actually be trying to suppress or deny it. (Of course 'being in denial' does not mean that the problem has gone away but that you are simply not dealing with it – and that is dangerous. It is like the alcoholic who refuses to admit that he is an alcoholic. That denial does not stop him drinking and destroying his life.)

SPONTANEOUS PROBLEMS ARISING ONE AT A TIME

Let your problems rise up spontaneously from within, like bubbles from the bottom of a bottle. You do not have to 'think' them up; they will come of their own accord if you give them time. There will be big and little problems, ones that have been there for only hours and ones that have been there years. Treat them all with the same care. You are going to try momentarily to take a short break from them so you can get a rest.

PLACING THEM ASIDE

As each problem comes up, see if you can place it next to you for a minute. Tell the problem that you will come back to it in a moment; it usually does not mind being placed outside if it knows that it is not being abandoned forever.

For example, you may have a bad feeling that you have been neglecting a close friend or relative for some time and this has been on your mind and getting in the way of your feeling really good about yourself. You feel you should contact them but 'just can't get round to it'.

Gently see if you can pick that feeling up as if it were a fragile vase, and put it down for a moment just next to you. If you cannot 'pick it up' try momentarily 'turning it down' as you would the gas under a boiling pot; or 'putting it on pause' as you would a tape or a video. Anything that will give both 'you' and 'it' a momentary rest from one another.

PLACING THE PROBLEM OUTSIDE

It does not really matter where you place the problem as long as you place it somewhere outside yourself and get a moment's relief from it.

Here are some suggestions of where you might put the problem; try any of them:

- on a soft pillow next to you
- on the ground
- on a shelf

- outside the door
- across the street
- on the other side of a river or a house or a hill or mountain

Try these suggestions till you find one that works.

GETTING DISTANCE

Remember the research findings – getting a safe distance from your problems means that they no longer overwhelm you. You can now see them and start to deal with them. When they totally overwhelm you, you cannot even begin to deal with them because you cannot see them clearly.

GETTING A DISTANCE FROM MY PROBLEMS BY PLACING THEM OUTSIDE MYSELF

STACKING YOUR PROBLEMS

You may find that you have several problems or issues that are getting in the way of your feeling really good right now. Take them one at a time and place them outside or stack them on a shelf next to you. Say the first problem that comes up is a row you had with your husband this morning. See if you can gently place it outside for a moment.

• Problem 1 placed outside: my husband

Then go back inside and see if that was the only problem that was on your mind. Ask yourself: 'Apart from that row with my husband, am I feeling OK inside?' Wait a minute and see if all feels well. If not, another problem will surface; for example, 'That parking ticket I did not pay and now I may get a £50 fine!' See if you can take that and place it gently outside you.

• Problem 2 placed outside: my parking fine

Go back and check again. Is everything feeling well inside now with your two problems placed outside? Give it thirty seconds to see how the centre of your body is. Perhaps there is another issue that starts to come up, weaving a knot of anxiety in your stomach. This time it's a 'biggie' and an 'oldie' – that problem you always seem to be having in relationships; the one where you are always 'giving in to him'.

This is a painful one and it seems to go right back to your relationship with your mother. And it also seems insoluble – constantly draining your energy and messing up your relationships. This is a dodgy and fragile one, and must be handled with care. If you can't place it outside yourself (it may be too 'big' a problem for that) see if you can take a couple of steps back from it – just to get some distance between you and 'it'.

• Problem 3 placed outside: my 'giving in to him' problem

Keep going till you have got some space from all your current problems. You will know this when you check inside and it feels OK and there are no other problems to stack.

It is not uncommon to have to stack five or six problems outside yourself before you get relief and feel OK inside.

Now try placing your problems outside for a minute.

Problem	Where placed
1	
2	
3	
4	
5	
6	

SAVOURING THE PEACE INSIDE

Now you have momentarily put aside your current set of problems, take a moment to enjoy how it feels inside without them. Really take as long as you like to enjoy the feeling.

112

I AM COMPLETELY HAPPY – OR AM I?

If you are having difficulties with this exercise you can try this way of identifying and getting space from your problems. Imagine that you are totally relaxed inside and 'problem free'. Go down into the middle of yourself and say something like: 'I am completely happy!'

Then notice if your gut feelings agree with you. They probably will not! But rather they will provide you with a list of things that are getting in the way of your being totally happy.

There will be large and small things – from 'I got a parking ticket that I haven't paid' to 'that whole problem about my mother'. One has been with you a day while the other has been there a lifetime. And you are going to take a break momentarily from both. Stack them in the same way that we did above.

BENEFITS OF 'GETTING SPACE' FROM MY PROBLEMS

- It gets you to identify personal problems that are being carried in your body while perhaps being 'suppressed' by your head
- It allows you to 'get distance' from them, which is essential if you are to start dealing with them in an effective manner

CONCLUSION OF EXERCISE

When you have stacked or otherwise placed outside all of your main problems, take a moment to experience how it is to be fully (or even partially) problem free. It does not matter if you could not put all of your problems aside – you've made a start.

Take some time to enjoy it, as you would take a break from the busy office or house to walk around the park.

It gives your mind and body a momentary relief in which it can recover.

Don't worry - your problems will be waiting for you when you get back to the office! But at least you will feel a bit more refreshed and perhaps a little better able to deal with them.

In the next stage of our Focusing work we are going to begin the process of resolving the core issues of the problem.

13

FOCUSING EXERCISE 5
FOCUSING ON ONE PROBLEM

Now you have learnt how to identify and get distance from bodily felt problems, you can start to focus on them. This will begin the inner process through which the problem is allowed to tell its story and heal.

You can use this exercise when you want to guide yourself or others through a full Focusing session. Professor Gendlin must be thanked for defining and testing these steps over many years of vigorous research at the University of Chicago. Through his work he helped make the Focusing process readily available to all.

THE SETTING FOR FOCUSING

Find a quiet place where you will not be interrupted. If you are sharing Focusing time with a partner, have a clock so that you can keep an eye on the time.

STEP 1: STACK ALL YOUR CURRENT PROBLEMS

Go over Focusing Exercise 3 again or use the quick recap

below to stack your current nagging worries or problems.

What's in the way of my feeling really happy right now?

Problem 1 is ...

Problem 2 is ...

Problem 3 is ...

Problem 4 is ...

Problem 5 is ...

Problem 6 is ...

etc ...

Take time to let your body disclose all the nagging problems it is carrying. Keep listing your current inner problems and placing them outside of you till you feel there are no more problems inside that have not been given the chance to rest outside.

Do not worry if you cannot identify all your problems exactly. You may only have a vague, uneasy feeling about something or someone – so just see if you can place that outside for a moment.

STEP 2: SELECT ONE PROBLEM FROM THE STACK

Let your body pick the most pressing problem, the one that needs attention right now. Lift it off the stack and bring it back inside you till you feel uptight or sad (or whatever it makes you feel).

As you bring it back into consciousness it will begin to make you feel tight or prickly (or whatever the feeling), just as bumping unexpectedly into someone you do not like makes your whole body 'prickle'!

This is the holistic gut or body 'feel' for the problem.

It is no longer just an idea in your head that you can rationalise or dismiss; you can actually feel it in your body. Now you can start to deal with or 'process' the problem.

STEP 3: GET A 'PICTURE' OR 'IMAGE' OF THE PROBLEM

As you focus your attention on the problem and really get a sense of how it 'feels' in your body, you may spontaneously get a 'picture' or 'photo' of it - an image or word that really sums up how it feels. This is your psyche 'seeing' the problem, perhaps for the first time, as it gets distance from it. Your psyche is now starting to work for you, forming a picture for you of the problem (which has until now been too close to 'see').

STEP 4: SHARP-FOCUS THE IMAGE TILL IT BECOMES CLEAR

Take the 'picture' of the problem - the word or image that sums it up - and compare it to the problem itself to see if it really does fit.

For example, a man who has a problem regarding his working relationship with an abusive colleague may describe the problem using the image of 'a tie that is so tight around my neck that I can hardly speak'.

But as he compares that image with the tight physical feeling in his throat when he thinks of this man, he finds that it does not fit. It is too weak an image. And as he focuses on the feeling in his neck, a better image comes - the image of 'a noose around my neck'.

STEP 5.1: FIRST QUESTION TO THE
PROBLEM FEELING
'WHAT'S THE WORST THING ABOUT ALL THIS?'

We communicate now with the problem itself and use the picture or word describing the problem to help us address the problem itself, e.g. 'What's the worst thing about this "noose around my neck" feeling?' This first question allows the often suppressed 'feeling of the problem' to get the chance of disclosing itself.

In the example of the man with the 'noose around his neck' feeling, the worst thing about it came to him after he had focused on it for a minute or so and it was: 'The realisation that I am actually too afraid to speak. I see that I cannot talk or express myself in any meaningful way when he is around; and as the success of my job depends on his cooperation, I sense that my inability to talk to him is actually endangering my job and livelihood. It is really quite sinister what he is up to. I also see that the pain in my throat results from my not saying anything to him when I should! And then I get mad at myself, knowing that I am a coward.'

Now try it yourself.

Ask your problem the following question (and use the image of the problem to help you get the answer): 'What's the worst thing about this whole problem?'

Wait a moment before you answer the question. In fact 'you' should not be answering the question at all! It is the job of that other part of your awareness - the Silent Watcher - to answer for you. When you have the answer, either write it down or spend a moment saying it to yourself out loud. If you do not make a point of saying it or recording it in some way, you will forget it.

The worst thing about this problem is ....
....

STEP 5.2: SECOND QUESTION TO THE PROBLEM FEELING
'WHAT NEEDS TO HAPPEN FOR THIS WHOLE THING TO BE SOLVED?'

The first question looked at the past of the problem. The second question looks at the future. What has to happen for the problem to be solved?

Here it is vital that you wait for the answer to come to you spontaneously. There is no point in thinking up the answer from your head – you've tried that many times already and you probably know in mind-bending detail what your head (and its inner critic) thinks.

What you are now waiting to hear is the voice of your genius – your inner Silent Watcher – the intuitive answer that comes directly to you, bypassing reason. The best way to ensure that you are listening to your spirit of genius and not your rational thought process is to focus on where the problem is *felt* in your body and look for the answer to come from there.

If it is felt in your gut – *focus* on your gut. If it is felt in your throat – *focus* on your throat.

When it comes it will be like a sudden flash of light-ning illuminating the problem. It will not be the same old stuff or advice you usually hear, but a fresh, clear and insightful voice that suddenly gives you a new outlook on the problem – a new feel about it.

You will feel a physical lightening of the problem in your body. It will be like the release of the physical tension – the sort you experience on suddenly finding your keys after frantically searching the house for them. You are pulling the place apart knowing you are going to miss a vital appointment when suddenly they turn up under a cushion on the sofa. The sense of relief is palpable and physically felt as a huge release of tension in the body. It is the same with the sudden insight that comes when your genius talks and shows you a way of dealing with an intractable emotional problem.

FOCUSING BREAKTHROUGH

Gendlin called this a 'felt shift'. The bodily tension associated with the problem shifts out of the body leaving a sense of calm and resolution. With that sudden intuitive inspiration, felt as a dramatic shift in the body's tension, comes an action step that arises out of the problem.

I can remember Gendlin saying in Chicago that the action step is the whole point of the process. A person is stuck and the body or its genius always provides an answer. It is an evolutionary prerogative. Nature cannot allow you – or life in whatever form – to stay 'stuck in the swamp' for long. It wants you to get on and achieve your potential.

For example, in the story above, the man who is being downtrodden at work waits for an answer to come from his Focusing question. When it does he feels it permeate his whole body. In his case it's a sudden insight: 'I am going to confront him! I am not going to lie down and die and let my job go – for I sense that is what he wants!' Once the clarity of intention is felt in the body, the stressful tension leaves and a sense of calm pervades the tissues.

You now have an action step that has come from your Focusing insight. Whether or not you take it is for you to decide.

DECISION TIME: WILL I ACT?

We now come to the central point in the Focusing process: will I act on the insight that comes to me? Will I take the action step that Focusing gives me? In other words, will I follow the advice of my Silent Watcher – the spirit of genius that is working inside on my behalf?

Always take a moment in silence to decide if you will act on this insight. It is your inherent and some would say divine right to exercise your freedom of will and choose one way or another. If you do decide to take the action step, work out the details (when, where, how etc.) and then, as the advert says: *just do it!*

Taking the Action Step

The whole point of the Focusing process – or any other therapeutic process – is now arrived at. In our example the man in the office decides to take the following action step: 'I will speak to him tomorrow at 11.10am when we have our coffee break. There will be no one around as our secretary is attending a training course. I will write down my main points in letter form and give him a copy and keep one for sending to our GM if things do not work out to my satisfaction.'

Once he has decided to take the action step, he feels better inside. Now he will have to depend on his courage and serendipity to help him through.

The Difficulty of Change

Never underestimate the difficulty of changing the status quo. Changing yourself often involves changing others (as our story shows), and you will meet with violent resistance on two fronts:
- from yourself, especially the part of you that is fearful, weak or just plain lazy
- from others who are used to your fearful, weak and

lazy side and who do not want the balance of power to change

Inner change can mean the end of certain outworn, cramping, abusive or negative relationships, and that will always involve great pain and grieving and even anger on all sides.

But change is never more painful than staying in stuck circumstances or relationships.

At the end of the day *we all decide one way or another* – even if it is to stay in abusive relationships. To paraphrase a great French philosopher: Wake up! Taste your freedom while you have it. But beware – many fall in love with their chains and the slave can come to love his master!

STEP 6: SAVOUR THE MOMENT AND THANK YOUR INSPIRATION

Always end by savouring the release and shift of tension that accompanies a sudden focused insight. Don't be too keen to rush back out into the stress of life. The insight that comes can soon be crushed by all your old conditioning and fears. It is important to:

- protect it from these reactionary forces within
- write down the insight and the action step or review it a couple of times during the day; otherwise you will forget both
- tell the problem that you will come back to it again soon
- keep your promise to take any action steps – your

Silent Watcher and your 'conscience' will not forget if you break a promise, and they can make life hell if you go back on a deal freely entered into!

In Conclusion

Congratulations – you have successfully focused! You can focus as often as the need arises, by yourself or with a partner. Every day if necessary. Focusing is not a once-off answer to one of life's problems but a continuous way of being with life's challenges. Use it and your insight and inspiration will grow.

Recap on the Six Steps

You can copy this set of guidelines on paper and paste it on cardboard, or stick it on a wall. Use it as a guide, but only after having mastered the previous Focusing exercises.

Step 1	Stack all your current problems
Step 2	Select one problem from the stack
Step 3	Get a 'picture' or 'image' of the problem
Step 4	Sharp-focus the image till it becomes clear
Step 5.1	First question to the problem feeling – 'What's the worst thing about this problem?'
Step 5.2	Second question to the problem feeling – 'What needs to happen for this whole thing to be solved?' Wait for the moment of focused inspiration and the answer to your problem

Step 6   Savour the moment and thank your
            inspiration

Now you might decide to go back inside and focus on
another problem in the stack, or you may decide you have
had enough for one day. Follow how your body feels.

TIPS ON FOCUSING

Focusing is not about fixing people's problems; it is about
allowing people to be with them in a certain useful way.

You can focus every day.

Early difficulties include imagining you have thought
up the answer in your head. The remedy here is to begin
relying on your gut and bodily felt feeling about the issue.
We have been programmed to live from the neck up and
we need help or training to get over this. Take classes or
courses in Focusing and listening (details at back).

The action step is all important. In the Law of Karma
we learn that in every problem there are a million possibilities open to us but only *one* that is perfectly suitable.
By feeling it in your body you will get an idea which is
the right one. Listen to your own genius – the angel of
your imagination and conscience.

Focusing and listening may be applied to all things and
in all relationships:
• love
• home
• friends
• work
It is about acting, not *re-acting*.

PART 3

LEARNING TO LISTEN

14

First Steps

Objective of listening: to help the person being heard to
get distance and space from their overwhelming problem.

Requirements: that the listener listens without passing
comment, giving advice or making a judgement.

In order to do this the listener must:

- listen quietly without interrupting
- show understanding by Focusing attention totally on
the person being heard
- use body language where appropriate to show understanding of what is being said (you will get good at
this over time – even if you think you will not)

It is easier to stay silent when first listening. If you are
going to speak, it is vital that you wait for the person to
stop speaking first. Then say back to them in their own
words what you have heard. Do not:

- advise
- comment

- talk about your experience
- reassure
- interrupt

SAFETY AND CONFIDENTIALITY

It is vital that you establish an atmosphere of complete trust and confidentiality. Never discuss what is said in listening sessions outside the session with anyone else. What takes place during listening is the 'speaker's process of self-discovery' and no one else's.

WHO DO I PICK TO LISTEN WITH?

Find a friend or colleague who is interested in this sort of self-discovery. Explain to them what you are trying to do, namely learn to listen to your own problems and help them resolve themselves. Give them a copy of this book; it will fill them in on what is going on.

Explain that you are going to share time together equally; you will either alternate sessions as listener/ hearer or split each section in half, so that you will each have, say, thirty minutes of listening followed by thirty minutes of being listened to.

Some people like to share listening time with a love partner, which can be very beneficial if the parties do not throw what comes up at each other in a row later on! Some people much prefer to listen with a friend or someone who is not too close to their lives. Trust your own intuition on this one.

SETTING

Somewhere mutually convenient that is:

- quiet
- comfortable
- interruption free
- not 'overheard'

ABOUT THESE LISTENING EXERCISES

These exercises have been well tested over more than thirty years of therapy and are used worldwide. I myself use them to teach groups and individuals the skills of empathetic listening. They really repay attention, and even though they may seem extraordinarily simple they are not!

In fact it is my experience that learning how to listen empathetically without interrupting, advising or reassuring is one of the most difficult skills human beings can learn. I have discovered that the very people who say, 'I'm a very good listener!' are usually the worst. What they actually mean is 'I'm very good at dispensing advice and fixing people's lives.'

But this is hardly surprising when you look at the controlled way most of us are brought up and the way we are ignored by adults (including our parents) when we are young. You are a lucky child indeed if you are treated as an equal human being who just happens to be small! The attitude that children 'should be seen and not heard' is still very prevalent. As children we were largely treated

130

as wild beings who would run off the rails unless strictly controlled; and the notion that a child could be wise would have been laughed at. As children we were told:

- how to behave
- what to believe
- how to believe it
- what to wear
- what to think

And if we rebelled we were called 'bad' or even 'evil' – depending on how strict our upbringing was. It was rarely that children were asked their opinion of things. It was supposed that they were merely blank books on which parents and teachers, priests and nuns could stamp their identity and authority. It is therefore hardly surprising that children who develop into young adults under these conditions should always be expecting to be told how they should live their lives.

The idea of becoming a self-actualising human being echoes Maslow's description of the ultimate state that human beings aspire to – becoming fully aware of themselves and their abilities. This would have found little favour in the controlled world of the young child. As a result, children and young adults can become dependent and self-doubting. The possibility of their possessing the answers to their own problems never even occurs to them.

THE DIFFICULTY OF REALLY LISTENING TO OTHERS

It is for this reason (and many others) that true non-directive and empathetic listening is very rare in our culture. Do not be surprised, when you start to listen empathetically, if you get the overwhelming urge to rush in and

- comfort
- direct
- interrupt
- share your own view
- get distracted

The only way around this is to *practise listening daily!*

15

___

LISTENING EXERCISE 1
SEEING HOW OTHERS DON'T LISTEN

LOOK AND LEARN

The best way to learn is to look around and experience it for yourself. This is called 'experiential' learning. In my first book, *Maximum Points - Minimum Panic*, I outlined the modern research approaches to learning, including how learning from experience is regarded as the most effective method. It proves that the best way to learn something is by doing it yourself.

So it is with listening skills. You must get out there and first see how people listen, or more commonly don't listen.

Start by looking around you. Go into

* a coffee shop
* a restaurant
* a pub
* a queue in a shop
* the post office
* the work canteen

- the kitchen at home

In fact anywhere and everywhere that people meet and talk. Notice how people

- talk
- listen
- interrupt
- go off at tangents of their own
- do not answer questions
- talk about themselves
- pass judgement
- freely dispense opinions and advice (usually poor!)
- do not concentrate on what the other person is saying

Notice in particular what happens when a person is talking about something personal and important, and how the other person reacts. For example, a woman begins discussing a personal problem she is having with her husband and how worried she is. Now notice how the other person reacts to this. According to the research, the listener will act in one of the following ways:

- interrupt and begin to talk about her own husband's behaviour
- tell the other person that things will be 'all right'
- tell the other person exactly what she 'should do about it!'
- ignore the other person's story altogether and talk about something else instead

RESEARCH INTO HOW WE DON'T LISTEN

Carl Rogers and his colleagues carried out a lot of research into how people don't listen. This research shows that in many so-called 'conversations' little exchange of ideas actually occurs. Neither is there much in-depth examination of personal issues. What actually happens is often as follows.

Let's say that a married man is worried about his wife. We will call him John. He's been busy and under pressure at work and for several weeks has tried to ignore the problem. Yet, as we have seen, ignoring a problem does not make it go away!

But he has been raised in a culture that does not encourage men to talk about emotional issues, so he has no idea where to start or even how to begin dealing with his highly personal problem. He meets his best friend Peter for a drink after work one night and decides he has to get this worry off his chest.

STRESS SYMPTOMS CARRIED IN THE BODY

As we have seen in our examination of Focusing and listening, John's body will be carrying the symptoms of the unresolved worry about his wife. He will be anxious, uptight, edgy and very possibly depressed. The symptoms are there as a warning to him that all is not well in his life, however hard he tries to pretend it is. The Silent Watcher inside is struggling to speak up and tell him that he needs to do something; his guiding spirit wishes to speak. We have seen that John now needs to focus or be listened to empathetically for this spirit to be heard inside. If it is, then four things will happen:

1 the Focusing will help make clear the vague 'worried' feeling inside, so he will find out what he is worrying about

2 from the clearer picture he will see where he is with this problem

3 the feelings of stress in his body at this unresolved issue will lift

4 he will have an action step and a direction that comes from inside himself and is congruent (whole) and true; he can now go on and do something about it

But for this to happen he must either be listened to empathetically or specifically focus on his problem. And unfortunately this does not often happen, as both Focusing and listening are still well-kept secrets – even to some psychologists and counsellors, let alone the vast majority of people.

So instead what usually happens is this.

UNMET NEEDS

John meets his friend in the hope that he can 'get something off his chest' and receive a bit of friendly advice. But his friend Peter has no idea of how to deal with emotional issues himself. He was never trained or even encouraged to talk about such things. His emotional intelligence quotient is therefore artificially low or barely existent. And as a result of this neglect he is acutely embarrassed at having to talk about anything remotely emotional. Therefore, the conversation develops as follows.

John begins to talk about his worry regarding his wife Sinead, and how they have not been talking or doing anything else together, including lovemaking, for the past two months.

At this stage Peter might well respond in one of the following ways:

- change the subject – the subject may just be too painful, embarrassing or awkward for Peter to handle and he might literally change the course of the conversation mid-stream and begin to talk about work as if nothing had been said. If you have ever had this happen to you, you will know just how disturbing an experience it is.
- reassure – Peter might reassure John with well-intentioned words like, 'I'm sure it's just a phase she's going through' or 'It happens to all couples at some time but she'll get over it!'
- interrupt John to talk about his own experience – Peter might jump in before John is finished and say something like, 'Me and Jane went through something of the sort a while back – but it just blew over. I'm sure it will for you' or 'Thank God! I never had that sort of problem with Jane. I think people give that sort of thing too much attention. Thankfully I'm not into all this "feely-feely" stuff!'

EFFECT ON JOHN

Just put yourself in poor John's shoes and see how he now feels. Not only has he been unable to explore the worry about his wife and get inner clarification by listening to his inner spirit, he now has a whole lot of advice and other people's stories, expectations and dismissals to cope with.

Instead of feeling freer inside (which would have happened if he had focused or been listened to, complete with an action step) he is now much worse off. The reason for this is that he will now have to bury and suppress the problem again, and not just for the evening with Peter while he talks about work and sport. He will probably find it more difficult when it comes to 'getting it off his chest' next time.

He drinks and smokes extra heavily that night to suppress the emotional worry and pain. When he gets home he cannot communicate any breakthrough to his wife. She is annoyed that he has been out all night drinking, and as they cannot communicate truly with each other, each imagines that the other is being cold and selfish and their problem deepens. Certainly she will not realise that John has made valiant efforts to remedy the situation.

APPALLED AT WHAT YOU HEAR

By looking around and listening to the way people communicate, you will see the terrible lack of training in this most basic of human skills. We often say that what makes us different from animals is our ability to talk. But we spend little or no time refining the skills of *listening* to what is said.

I am a university graduate with years of teaching experience and it was not until quite recently that I heard of Rogerian listening and Gendlin's Focusing. It was a complete mystery, as was the process of counselling, therapy and what psychotherapists, psychologists and psychiatrists actually did.

Before that I was totally ignorant of how to listen effectively and would spend hours in conversation with my pupils and friends doing the following:

- fixing their lives
- 'advising' them – or actually telling them what to do
- telling them how I have coped in my life with the same sort of problem
- telling them that they are silly to worry about the problem

They would thank me, take their leave and go off and do exactly as they would have done anyway! Advice has been proven to be largely a waste of time.

As a result of my experiences with Focusing and listening, I now sit back, shut my mouth and listen to them – and if I do open my mouth it is only to say back to them some of the things they have just said. And it works!

People come back and say things like, 'That chat was so useful. I did what I said I would and went to see Mary, and something is going to happen!' They may even add,

'Thanks for all your advice!'

But then I have to stop them and say, 'You did the work – I only listened. I gave you *no* advice!' Sometimes they don't believe that they thought up the advice for themselves! So I stop them again and explain what happens during listening: 'By being heard you have begun to listen to the voice of your own wisdom and to find a path out of your difficulties.'

Then I have often found myself asking: 'How could another short-sighted human being, caught up in time and space and living through his or her own very limited experience, possibly guide another person better than this profound inner personal guide that speaks to every individual?'

16

LISTENING EXERCISE 2
CAN YOU HEAR ME?

FIND A FRIEND

Find a friend, someone you like and trust, and tell them that you are learning how to focus and listen. Ask them if they will join you in a little experiment.

Now find a dilemma or problem that is facing you currently (this part is usually easy!). Make sure it is something that you feel you can talk about comfortably. It could be that you are worried about what to do with your ageing mother: should you stay with her in the house or help her find permanent care? Or you may be thinking of leaving a relationship or a job.

MEET UP

Arrange to meet and ask your friend to listen and react to your problem. Listen carefully to how they do this and analyse their reactions. Look for the following:

- Do they listen to you?
- If so, for how long?

How soon is it before they

- interrupt?
- advise you?
- talk about their own experience of a similar problem?
- tell you how they would deal with it?
- dismiss it as not being a problem?
- get bored?
- become anxious?
- become distracted?

Now ask yourself this question: 'Was I listened to in a way that allowed me to find my own solutions?'

TRY THIS WITH SEVERAL PEOPLE

Do your own research, asking several people. You may find that those you would expect to be good listeners, like priests, doctors, counsellors and teachers, are in fact the worst of all (unless they have done a good listening/counselling course). What they are good at - like most people - is telling you how you should live your life.

FINALLY

Add up the number of people who listened to you without advising you, analysing you, directing you or changing the subject and talking about themselves. If you found any who did none of the above, hold onto them – they are rare friends!

17

LISTENING EXERCISE 3
LISTENING IN SILENCE

Now you have done your research, you are going to see
if you can begin listening to people in a useful way.

LISTENING PARTNER

Ideally, it would be great if you could find a companion
who would like to become your listening partner, someone with whom you will share listening time.

SET-UP

Meet your listening partner and decide on a subject that
you are both comfortable with. On the first few occasions
the subject matter does not have to be anything very
personal. If you are having difficulty finding something
to talk about, choose a topic dear to your heart, like a
favourite childhood memory you have or a pastime you
enjoy; or any unfulfilled ambitions or a description of
someone close to you – what they are like and how they
make you feel.

Alternatively you can do Focusing Exercise 2 or 3, which will make you very aware of your body, and then talk about how you experienced that exercise. This has the advantage of being real and spontaneous. It also puts you in touch with the 'body feel' of your life, which is where Focusing and listening really start.

TALKING ABOUT REAL ISSUES

As you get more comfortable with the listening/talking routine, you will begin to feel able to talk about the real issues in your life and to explore your emotional inner world. But do not feel that you have to force the pace on this – it will happen of its own accord.

CHOOSE LISTENER/SPEAKER AND TIME FRAME

Decide who will talk first and roughly for how long. But always leave the time open as something may come up that will need extended attention. If you do have to end in the middle of something unfinished, always tell the issue that you will come back to it later, either on your own if it is urgent or next time you both meet. Surprisingly, issues (which have a life of their own) do quieten down if they get attention. It is only when they feel abandoned that they start to complain, triggering the stress response and filling the body with stress hormones.

Never leave delicate or painful issues cut-off and hanging in the air. Always make an appointment to return to them when it is convenient.

IF YOU ARE THE SPEAKER

Remember that it is usual to be self-conscious on the first couple of occasions when speaking. But that's OK. Stick at it and soon you'll find that you are not so self-conscious but more self-aware – which is a pleasant feeling.

In no time at all you may find that you really enjoy speaking and being heard. It holds the mirror of insight up to you and you begin to see things that you never saw in yourself before.

WORRYING ABOUT THE LISTENER

You may find you are worried that the listener must be getting bored with you. But while respecting this fear, try to move on. We become so used to being available to others that we sometimes feel guilty about giving time to ourselves. Your guilty feeling may be part of your problem – so give it attention.

Anyway, you will be switching roles and becoming the listener in a while, so don't feel too bad!

WHAT IF I HAVE NOTHING TO SAY?

First understand that this is a common early problem in being heard. We are so used to being interrupted and dissected that this sudden unfamiliar silence can be freaky! Try to live with it or bring attention to the uncomfortable feeling and see if you can speak about it. It could link you in to something inside you that needs attention.

For example: 'I feel really awkward right now. I can't think of anything to say and I'm sure I must be boring you.'

Even speaking about it will often help the awkward feeling by relieving the pressure. In addition you are now talking about your inability to talk. This could be a rich area for you to explore. And it may well be that this part of you – the part that feels awkward and boring – itself needs attention.

IF YOU ARE THE LISTENER

On this first occasion we will make it easier for you by just getting you to listen in silence. Simply show that you understand what your partner is saying by

- nodding
- using your eyes
- saying words like 'Yes' or 'I see'

All that is needed is for you to be really present for your listening partner and to give him or her your full attention. That is enough.

SUM UP WHAT HAS BEEN SAID

At the end of the exercise you can briefly sum up what the speaker has said in a couple of sentences using his or her own words. This will help your partner see his or her feelings clearly, as in a mirror. You can also briefly discuss how the speaking/listening went for you both. When this is done swap around. Now let's do the exercise.

START OF LISTENING EXERCISE 3
LISTENING IN SILENCE

This is a simple exercise but surprisingly demanding to do.

- Allocate the time, say five minutes each for the first session. (Add five minutes to each subsequent session till you listen/speak for thirty minutes each.)
- If you are the speaker, talk about whatever you want for five minutes.
- If you are the listener, listen with total attention for five minutes and show that you understand by using body language and eye contact. At the end of the five minutes, sum up briefly what you heard the speaker say - using the speaker's words as much as possible.
- Discuss how you both felt and any difficulties or awkwardness you encountered. (There will be some!) Then swap roles and repeat the whole procedure.

Well done - you have just completed your first listening/ speaking session. It may not have felt much and it may have been awkward, but you are on the road to learning the highly effective skill of empathetic listening. Keep trying this exercise until you are comfortable with the process.

18

LISTENING EXERCISE 4
REFLECTING

The next exercise is the same as Exercise 3 but with 'reflective listening' incorporated.

REFLECTIVE LISTENING

This is when you allow the person to speak and then you reflect or say back to the person what you have just heard, using wherever possible the same words that the person used. For example:

Speaker: When I think about the relationship I just cannot make up my mind if it should keep on going. On the one hand I find that he is such a terrific support and that he is good and kind in so many ways – he really helps my life feel better. (pause) But part of me really thinks that we are not compatible at all. I see some others guys at the office and I know we get on better intellectually and socially. I feel more comfortable just talking to them . . . they're much more 'me'! But then it breaks my heart to think of leaving the comfort of this man. It's like I cannot face the pain that that will cause him *and* me!

Listener: So it's like you really like this man and the way he brings comfort to your life. But there is also a part that sees other guys at the office and how well you get on with them socially and intellectually, how they're more 'you'. But you don't want to split with your partner because of the hurt it will cause both of you.

This reflection, far from boring the speaker, will actually fascinate her, in the same way as we are fascinated by our reflection in the mirror and will look at it intently (just as we always look first at ourselves in group photos and are fascinated – and often horrified! – at the way we look). There is a part of us that is fascinated by ourselves and seems to be detached from and able to look at us. This is an aspect of the Silent Watcher.

THE SILENT WATCHER

We have talked about this part – the Silent Watcher that observes us as we live and struggle to make decisions.

When what we say is reflected back, we get to stand outside ourselves and see a verbal reflection of ourselves. Suddenly, instead of 'being' and 'acting', we are looking at ourselves 'being' and 'acting'. It is a completely different experience and gives us a totally different perspective.

It seems that we see the Silent Watcher more clearly in this reflective mirror and hear what he has to say. Then

150

we can begin to fine-tune the image of what we now see, like a person adjusting a tie in the mirror. It may even be that we change some of the opinions we have formed – just as we may decide to change a jacket or tie when we look in the mirror and see how terrible they really look! The act of reflection is very useful for helping us see what we really think and feel.

REFLECTIVE LISTENING ALLOWS US TO 'SEE OURSELVES'

151

ADJUSTMENTS AS THE PERSON 'SEES' HERSELF IN THE REFLECTIVE MIRROR

As people 'hear back' what they have just said, they may find on reflection that it is not what they really feel inside after all. Just as we may be convinced that a certain jacket looks really well on us until we see it in the mirror and go 'Ugghh!'

Reflective listening gives us the chance to reflect and see from a distance how the feeling sits on us. If we find on reflection that it does not sit well we will change it to something that does. As in this example (continued from above):

> *Listener:* But you don't want to split with your partner because of the hurt it will cause both of you.
> *Speaker:* (pauses while reflecting on this) No! That's not true! It's not his pain I'm concerned about at all – it's mine! Part of me is really terrified of being alone. Say I leave him and ... no one wants me ... The truth of it is I don't want to be on my own.

THE 'INSIGHT' OR 'REVELATION'

A sudden insight or revelation can come at any time during reflective listening; and the important thing is that it is self-realised. This is where reflective listening is so useful, helping the you see the truth about your own life. This realisation is entirely different from having someone tell you what they think about you.

152

Let's say that John is told by Bill that he is staying in a relationship with Jane for his own selfish reasons – what happens then? The listener (Bill) will only have made the speaker (John) feel defensive, judged and bad. This will have had the effect of isolating John and making the truth even more difficult to face. Telling people that they are selfish and self-deluding may be true – but it can also be very counterproductive and destructive.

When the truth is felt and seen from within, however, something useful can happen.

THE USEFULNESS OF THE 'TRUTH'

Eugene Gendlin wrote the following in his book *Focusing*:

> What is true is already so. Owning up to it doesn't make it worse. Not being open about it doesn't make it go away. And because it's true, it is what is there to be interacted with. Anything untrue isn't here to be lived. People can stand what is true, for they are already enduring it.

The truth is reality. It is what is real. If we want to build a house we must know the truth about the ground on which it is to be built. We must know the composition of the soil and the depth at which rock starts. If we do not know, or if we kid ourselves that there is rock there but instead there is sand, then our house will collapse. It will literally have been built on a lie.

The truth is useful. It is essential if we are to make sound decisions involving ourselves and others. Reflective listening is a way in which individuals come to see their own truth and so make sound decisions.

There are two ways in which you can listen reflectively: the short method and the long method.

THE SHORT METHOD OF REFLECTIVE LISTENING

Never interrupt, let the speaker finish his or her sentence, and then select and reflect a key 'feeling' word or words.

For example, Paula is in a difficult relationship with a man called Alan:

> *Paula*: It's so difficult saying anything to Alan. He gets so aggressive and the whole evening is ruined while he has one of his fits. I often go to say something to him and it's there – right on the tip of my tongue – but I bite it back. I just can't face the hassle.
> *Listener*: You can't face hassle.

The speaker hears this mirrored back and as a consequence goes deeper into examining her feelings.

> *Paula*: No, I can't take it ... I just seem to fold inside ... I don't have the stomach for it anymore. Maybe I'm a coward?
> *Listener*: A coward?

The speaker again pauses for a moment as she weighs and measures this single reflected word 'coward'. Inside she is considering for the first time whether she is a coward.

154

Already the emphasis has changed from her volatile partner and his behaviour, to her own and her possible cowardice. She reflects and then continues:

> *Paula*: Yeah, maybe I'm a coward after all ... The bastard shouldn't get away with it but I let him – and I didn't always ... (ponders on this)
> *Listener*: You didn't.

The speaker is now allowed by this reflective listening to go deep into her memory of a time when she did not accept such behaviour from her partner. She pauses as she reflects on this, lost for a moment in thought. *It is vital that the listener does not interrupt her here!*

He doesn't, and instead keeps his eyes on her, giving her his full, silent attention. After a moment she speaks, but her voice now is quieter and more serious.

> *Paula*: No I didn't ... not at all. He was very polite then, he treated me well – with respect ... but somehow I had more respect for myself. (lifts her head and looks at her companion with eyes that appear to have just realised something) I definitely had more respect for myself ... but somehow I've lost it ...
> *Listener*: You've lost it?
> *Paula*: (looking back at her companion, a growing realisation in her eyes) Yes, definitely! I've lost respect for myself and that's allowing him to treat me like that ...
> *Listener*: It is?

Paula: Yeaah ... perhaps I'm causing him to treat me like that! (laughs gently as this new realisation dawns on her)

It is interesting to see what goes on during reflective listening as opposed to the usual form of verbal intercourse, as revealed by Rogers's research.

The woman could have got into a good conversational argument if the listener had engaged her in conversation rather than pure listening. Then she would not have begun to get into such deep personal insights and to explore such possibilities concerning her behaviour and feelings. She would have had a generalised conversation about the way men treat women. Or she could have got into a tirade about his treatment of her, which could also have developed into a generalised conversation about how men treat women.

But as she was listened to she was able to switch to her own behaviour, which is something she can do something about. She can eventually fix herself (with difficulty), whereas there is no guarantee that she can fix him.

She was able to hear back her assumptions and as a consequence challenge and throw some of them out. For example, she began to see that it was her behaviour rather than his that was the cause of his attitude to her.

Had empathetic listening *not* taken place:

- Paula would probably never have reached such a point of understanding of her own behaviour
- the focus of attention would not have been on her

- she would not have addressed her own attitude to her partner to the same extent
- she would not have got an understanding as to what she could now do to remedy the situation

In this case, the short method of reflective listening was used: all it required was the reflection of *one or two key words* for Paula to have the mirror held up to her feelings.

COMMON RESPONSES TO WHAT PEOPLE SAY

Most people would answer an emotional statement, like Paula's in the example above, in one or more of the following ways:

- with well-intentioned sympathy: 'That's dreadful for you!'
- with judgement: 'The selfish bastard!'
- with their own story: 'My John does exactly the same!'
- with advice: 'You'll have to stand up to him!'

Research shows that none of these work – they don't change anything!

The short reflective listening response allows the person to get a picture of her own behaviour for herself. She may then go on to see another layer of the truth about herself.

USE SHORT 'FEELING' WORDS

When using this short form of listening, focus in on the

'feeling' words that really catch the emotion of what is being said, e.g.:

- 'I feel so sad.'
- 'I am weary of the whole thing now.'
- 'I only have to look at him to feel mad.'

It is the *feeling words* that catch the whole mood of the person.

THE LONG METHOD OF REFLECTIVE LISTENING

Let's go back to an earlier extract for an example of the long method of reflective listening.

> *Speaker:* When I think about the relationship I just cannot make up my mind if it should keep on going. On the one hand I find that he is such a terrific support and that he is good and kind in so many ways – he really helps my life feel better. (pause) But part of me really thinks that we are not compatible at all. I see some other guys at the office and I know we get on better intellectually and socially. I feel more comfortable just talking to them . . . they're much more 'me'! But then it breaks my heart to think of leaving the comfort of this man. It's like I cannot face the pain that that will cause him *and* me!
>
> *Listener:* So it's like you really like this man and the way he brings comfort to your life. But there is also a part that sees other guys at the office and how

well you get on with them socially and intellectually, how they're more 'you'. But you don't want
to split with your partner because of the hurt it will
cause both of you.

Here there are a lot of points all contained within one long
speech – and they are all important. It is vital to be able
to say the key points back, so the speaker can see the
logic of her own thoughts. And as we saw earlier, this
'mirroring' leads to an important insight on the part of
the speaker:

> *Speaker.* No! That's not true! It's not his pain I'm
> concerned about at all – it's mine! Part of me is
> really terrified of being alone. Say I leave him
> and . . . no one wants me . . . The truth of it is I don't
> want to be on my own.

HOW TO GIVE LONG FORM REFLECTIVE LISTENING

You only get good at this sort of listening by lots of
practice. Try some of the following tips:

- practise summing up the main points of arguments
  with a friend or someone being interviewed on a radio
  or TV chat show
- listen to people in buses, restaurants and pubs and
  start to see how they put their sentences together; try
  to précis what they say
- when you are next with a friend or colleague try
  listening to them in this way and see if you can sum

up what they have said without telling them that you
are learning to listen

Everybody loves to be heard. Try it and see!

19

LISTENING EXERCISE 5
LISTENING PARTNERSHIPS

LISTENING PARTNERSHIPS - EXERCISE FOR THE SOUL

In America, the home of listening and Focusing, people are beginning to see them as processes that need to be undertaken regularly. It's no longer the case that you go into therapy, get a problem sorted out and then start living. Nowadays, people are seeing that the problem of living never goes away – any more than sickness and human infirmity go away. You don't do a fitness programme for three months and then presume that you will be fit for the rest of your life. So it is for the human psyche. It too needs to be regularly attended to and exercised.

THE 'SOUL WORKOUT'

At first it may need special help (just as a medical check-up and a supervised fitness programme are recommended for people who are completely out of shape).

Most people are never really taught how to attend to the health of their psyche (the Greek word for 'soul') and as a consequence they neglect it and end up spiritually sick or unfit. It used to be the job of the churches to look after the soul, but recent research shows that a growing number of people are finding themselves cut off from established religion. They find that their needs are no longer being met by traditional religious practice. But those needs are still there and they still need attending to – especially in our highly materialistic world. Nowadays it seems that behavioural science and the work of people like Jung, Rogers and Gendlin are showing us the ways in which the soul functions and how we can meet its many complex needs.

Personally, I have found profound spiritual insight and comfort in practising listening and Focusing. What could be more spiritual than listening to someone else's torn heart without judgement and with unconditional attention (which is another word for *love*) so that the person gets an inner enlightenment and healing and an answer to their problems that seems to come from a source connected to themselves.

I would go further and say that Focusing and listening can be seen as the process whereby the body meets what we used to call *spirit* and *soul*. I have certainly felt this and do not now need to rely so much on formal prayer to answer my problems; I can hear the mysterious voice of my spirit whispering inside my soul. When I meet someone who is in need I now have a very real way of helping them – I listen; and from this process they derive real and congruent help that is as profound as it is lasting.

'STRESSED OUT' PEOPLE

In my job I see and work with 'stressed out' people who
have been through every sort of help available – from CAT
scans of their brains to ECGs of their 'stressed' hearts.
They have often been through the hands of the best
doctors, psychiatrists and psychologists and tried every
form of behavioural and chemical treatment without
noticeable long-term help. They often only come to me –
in my capacity as a stress consultant – as a last resort
after being told, 'There's nothing wrong with you – you're
just stressed out! Learn to relax and switch off!' And so
they come to me to learn to relax.

And all that I do is make a space for them where they
can say what they want and be as they want to be. And I
listen to them empathetically and teach them the Focusing
skills. After only two or three sessions of this sort of
focused and listening attention, they get in touch with
themselves in a way that is very powerful, and I hear them
say things like, 'For the first time in years I really saw what
the problem was and I got a sense of release that I have not
felt in ages.' And they go off and start to do things on their
own to remedy the situation. I have such admiration for
these people who have finally found a way of being with
themselves and of helping themselves. It is then that I see
just how powerfully effective Rogers's and Gendlin's discoveries are – how they actually add to the lives of people
by giving them tools that actually work, putting them
directly in touch with their guiding awareness within, and
giving them back a sense of self-empowerment.

LISTENING PARTNERSHIPS

I would really encourage you to form a listening and Focusing relationship with a close friend or colleague. It will allow you to get in touch with that special awareness and the force that wants what is best for you.

And if you do form such a partnership, you will come to understand not just yourself but another human being in a way that is very special. At the outset you should:

- decide a time and place that suits you both, or alternate, say between your place and theirs, if you are doing it from a home base
- agree to share time equally, e.g. this week for you to be heard and next week for them

RECAP ON EMPATHETIC LISTENING

- listen in silence and nod or say 'Yes' or 'I see'
- never interrupt
- use your body language to show you understand
- give your partner total attention
- never discuss personal details with other people
- most important of all – do not interpret, analyse or pass comment on what they say

At the end of each session you can discuss: (a) how you felt being heard and/or (b) what you learned as the listener.

20

LISTENING TO THE WORLD

You can go on and give listening time to everyone you meet. You will be pleasantly surprised at what you learn about human nature. Try listening to your

- partner
- son or daughter
- mother and father
- sister and brother
- friend
- work colleagues
- the strangers life brings your way

LISTENING – ITS GLOBAL SIGNIFICANCE

Perhaps we will soon find that listening is central to solving the global problems that humanity faces. If man can listen to himself then perhaps he can begin to listen to the troubled and endangered world he lives in.

COMMON PROBLEMS WHEN TRYING TO LISTEN

The following are some of the problems that you will encounter when trying to listen to others. First comes a huge desire to:

- interrupt
- analyse
- interpret
- advise
- correct
- otherwise change what the person is *feeling*

And people who are facing problems and change are sorely tempted to do the following with their problems:

- suppress them
- deny they exist at all
- replace them with 'positive thoughts' or addictive religious practice – both of which can be massive forms of denial
- distract themselves by getting 'busy'
- do anything that stops them from processing the problem all the way to a full, bodily felt resolution

PROCESSING THE PAIN

Behavioural science has shown us that pain of whatever kind needs to be processed if it is to resolve itself and heal. It was Kubler-Ross who first discovered that the only way to heal a serious bereavement was to experience fully the stages of grief; only then could you come to full acceptance and healing. Skip even one painful stage and the process could get stuck.

Pain, once it is experienced fully, dissipates naturally, because the organism has gone through the pain and mended itself, just as a broken bone does when it is set.

FEELING THE PAIN FULLY IN YOUR BODY

Kubler-Ross emphasised that the main ingredient in recovery was to experience fully the painful feelings in the body. Only then could full resolution be achieved.

Taking tablets, drinking, denying or fleeing the pain delayed recovery and made the person sink even deeper into their grief. The way to help recovery was to listen to the person and help them experience their pain fully.

It is the same with Focusing and listening. Here we focus our attention on the emotional discomfort within, be it stress or anxiety or panic. It is by addressing the pain and giving it attention that we find the solution.

THE PROCESS LOOKS AFTER ITSELF

Once the process starts, it looks after itself and brings the person to resolution. This is where the sense of grace is most clearly found, a force or guiding spirit that looks after people who are troubled; binding their wounds and showing them the way to full recovery. And this spirit is freely found within and does not have to be bought! It is always there and it always answers.

But don't take my word for it – try it yourself and see!

EPILOGUE: BECOMING A GENIUS

ACCESSING YOUR EMOTIONAL INTELLIGENCE

Focusing and listening put you in touch with the part of you that knows what you uniquely need. The research of Gendlin and Rogers shows that we have in our psyche a near infallible guide. It's as if the psyche contained a psychological immune system that addressed emotional problems, taking us beyond time and space, helping us to be inspired and intuitive.

I have a feeling that Gendlin and Rogers have actually discovered the workings of conscience.

GETTING WELL AGAIN
WHAT FOCUSING AND LISTENING WILL DO FOR YOU

Focusing and listening are pure forms of natural therapy. Therapy means 'treatment' and the research shows that Focusing and listening are the ways in which we should normally and naturally treat our bodies.

For Focusing and listening produce a gentle and tolerant internal atmosphere in which things can be heard and allowed to express themselves, especially all those things that our conditioning says should be suppressed.

168

They also let us get in touch with all the lies that we were told and that we believed because we were too young to know any better: things like 'I'm stupid' or 'selfish' or 'ugly' or 'bad' or 'sinful' or 'unwanted'. It allows these lies to be exposed like a virus and laid open to the attacks of our own natural psychological immune system.

SELF-THERAPY
RELYING ON THE SACRED INNER TRUTH

Focusing and listening also allow us to break away from the 'Myth of the White Coat', the idea that someone else knows the answer to our problems – be it a psychologist, doctor, counsellor or priest. It brings to mind the assertion made in the Gospel, that the true 'counsellor' is the spirit of truth within you, and that 'The kingdom of God is within.'

As we have said elsewhere, the voice of inspiration is a sacred voice. And leaving the chains of our conditioning behind is perhaps the art of growing to maturity. Making up the links in the conditioning chains are the assumptions that figures of authority – those wearing the white coats and white collars – know things we don't and are in a position to tell us how to lead our lives. This is clearly not the case, but sometimes we believe it. We need to hack off our chains, and this often leaves raw and exposed tissue and bones.

It takes courage to cast them off, but that is the challenge of true adulthood.

LISTENING TO THE CUT-OFF PARTS OF ME

In this new form of self-therapy, we will be able to take charge of our own process and listen to the cut-off and rejected parts of our psyche. Then we will be able to hear its story and see, perhaps for the first time in years, just how wounded it is and why it acted as it did – which was often in order to protect us when we were vulnerable and young.

BEING 'TOO CARING'

It is interesting to note that one of the criticisms that was levelled at Carl Rogers's work was that it was 'too gentle and caring'. Some therapists argued that as the world was harsh and unkind, it was unsuitable to have a therapy that got people used to being heard *unconditionally*. The reason they gave was that people would be disappointed when they returned from their therapy and entered the 'real world' with all its cruelty.

This is a bit like saying that nobody should be loved because the world out there is unloving; or that nobody should be kind because the world out there is unkind. If that were true the Gospel of love and forgiveness would not be heeded lest people be disappointed when they entered the real world and found hatred or indifference.

THERAPY AS IT SHOULD BE

One could really say that being treated with respect – as people are in the Focusing and listening environment –

is how we are designed to be treated in the world. The fact that the world has got it wrong in no way undermines the validity, and indeed the necessity, of being caring and compassionate.

Treating people in a Focusing/listening way – also called the 'client centred' or 'person centred' approach – is natural and right. If we did this daily we would start to produce congruent, self-aware and responsible people (responsible meaning having the *ability to respond*).

We would also have people who would not split off from themselves, and people who could listen to themselves and others, with all their inspirations, intuitions, insights and dreams.

BENEFITS OF FOCUSING AND LISTENING

The benefits of Focusing and listening are well researched and clinically proven. They include:

- psychological congruence
- resolution of short and long term emotional problems
- resolution of other problems, including creative, business, writing and planning
- alleviation of pain
- development of intra-personal or emotional intelligence
- improvement in the condition of those suffering from stress-affected illnesses, including heart disease, cancer and high blood pressure
- alleviation of depression by attending to the psychological and emotional problems that contribute to it

- development of interpersonal intelligence
- development of a relationship with yourself
- development of relationships with other people including a lover, family, friends, work colleagues and neighbours

HEALING THE WORLD

From all this Focusing and listening comes a natural empathy and an insight into how our fellow human beings are feeling. We can hear more clearly their pain and see exactly what it is like to live in their skins. There is a saying of the American Indians: 'Walk in your enemy's shoes for a day and you will pity rather than hate him.'

But most of all you will be opening the split-off, damaged part of yourself to reintegration and redemption.

ARE YOU DISINTEGRATING?

It has been said that there are only two states in life: integration and disintegration. It would be interesting to check and see which path your own life is following – the path of integration or that of disintegration?

The work of integrating the split-off parts of yourself is sacred work. The great philosopher Carl Jung said that redeeming the damaged, disintegrated and dark side of our personalities is the greatest work we can do in life. For only from our own personal redemption or reintegration can come the redemption and reintegration of our fractured world.

A FINAL WORD ON 'EVERYDAY GENIUS'

Focusing and listening are like standing on the threshold of our own internal chaos and listening to the primordial sounds within – the sounds of our souls. And perhaps the sound of chaos that echoes in our souls is but the distant echo of that original moment of creation, when the universe exploded into existence with a bang that is still heard today. But we do not yet know if the Big Bang was a moment of creation or one of destruction. Was it the creation of all matter or the fall from grace of Lucifer or mankind? And are we here to create from scratch or to repair the wounds of this original Fall?

Whatever the answer, it is here that we must stand – right on the threshold of this primordial chaos – if we are to hear the answers that we need. For out of the chaos comes symmetry and design.

It is as if a messenger had winged its way across the chaotic abyss to deliver its message right into the heart of man's understanding – his soul. And this message helps us to live as we are designed to live. Not in head but in heart, listening to the inner voice. And perhaps if we listen closely and carefully enough to the messenger we will find out the answers we are so desperately looking for in the core of our beings – in bodies and souls made up of the very stardust that came into existence at that moment of creation.

It seems that part of the point of life is to discover why we were given life. In order to solve that great mystery – one that transcends both time and space – we may need help from beyond time and space. Focusing may be the art of listening to that timeless help. When we focus and listen we are hearing the voice of the timeless guide who whispers within us.

It may well be, after all, that the Romans were right, and that we are all given a guiding spirit at birth – the spirit of our genius. It is there to help us through this life and – according to the Romans – to guide us into the next.

Good luck on your journey! It is often a hard one – but it is the only one we have. And perhaps we get more help on the way than we think.

What is more, we don't have to struggle or beg, bargain or implore for this kind of help. It is there all the time. We only have to turn inward and listen to the silence within . . . and there, after a moment, we will hear the voice of our ever-watchful guide, our own unique *genius*. It is a voice that is quiet and gentle; one that is always on our side. It is the voice that provides answers to our innermost problems and worries, the voice of guidance and help – and perhaps, as some have thought, it is the voice of our angel, whispering to us in the pregnant silence that exists between our thoughts.

FURTHER READING

If you are interested in any of the subjects touched on in this book and wish to pursue them you may find the following selection of titles of interest.

Gendlin, Eugene T. *Focusing*. Bantam Press, new ed. 1997.

Gendlin, Eugene T. *Focusing Orientated Psychotherapy*. Guilford Press, 1996.

Rogers, Carl. *On Becoming a Person*. Constable, 1974.

McMahon, Ed. *Beyond the Myth of Dominance*. Sheed and Ward, 1993.

Wieser Cornell, Anne. *The Power of Focusing*. New Harbinger Publications, 1996.

Goleman, Daniel. *Emotional Intelligence*. Bloomsbury Publications, 1996.

Chopra, Deepak. *Quantum Healing*. Bantam Press, 1989.

Siegel, Bernie. *Love, Medicine and Miracles*. Rider, 1986.

Dossey, Larry. *Healing Words*. Harper Collins, 1993.

FURTHER INFORMATION

An audio tape to accompany this book is available from
Kevin Flanagan at the address below, priced at £7.99
(including postage and packaging). A tape of his first
book, *Maximum Points - Minimum Panic*, the bestselling
guide to passing exams, is available at £6.99.

Kevin Flanagan
2 Leeson Walk
Northbrook Road
Dublin 6
Tel: 01-496 5202; e-mail: kevinflanagan@tinet.ie

Kevin Flanagan conducts

- one-on-one introductory Focusing sessions
- a two-year Focusing teacher training course leading to
  certification with the Focusing Institute in New York
  – this course qualifies people to teach Focusing
- the Professional Stress Management Course, held over
  two weekends, leading to ITEC certification

He also gives lectures on stress and Focusing in schools,
colleges and businesses.

Everyday Genius (£7.99 incl. p&p) and *Maximum Points
- Minimum Panic* (£6.99 incl. p&p) are available in all
bookshops or may be ordered direct from the Mercier
Bookshop, PO Box 5, 5 French Church Street, Cork.